CLEMSON
CROWNED

Head coach Dabo Swinney hugs his wife Kathleen on the trophy stand as Clemson celebrates its national championship victory over Alabama. The Tigers defeated the Crimson Tide 35-31 to win the 2016 title in Tampa. (Bart Boatwright/The Greenville News)

This book is available in quantity at special discounts for your group or organization.
For further information, contact:

Triumph Books LLC
814 North Franklin Street
Chicago, Illinois 60610
Phone: (312) 337-0747
www.triumphbooks.com

Printed in U.S.A.
ISBN: 978-1-62937-296-9

The Greenville News/Anderson Independent Mail
Katrice Hardy VP / Executive Editor / Southeast Regional Editor
Bill Fox / Managing Editor
Steve Bruss / News Director
Jim Rice / Sports Editor
Kathy Nelson / Interim Sports Editor
Photographers: Bart Boatwright, Ken Ruinard
Reporters: Brad Senkiw, Scott Keepfer, Manie Robinson and Dan Hope

Content packaged by Mojo Media, Inc.
Joe Funk: Editor
Jason Hinman: Creative Director

Front and back cover photos by Bart Boatwright/The Greenville News.

Bart Boatwright/The Greenville News

CONTENTS

INTRODUCTION

By Jim Rice

y memories of Clemson University's 1981 national championship season are pretty much highlighted by two days in 1982.

On Jan. 1, I watched every moment of the Orange Bowl.

About a week later, I interviewed Tony Berryhill, the 216-pound starting center on the championship team for his hometown newspaper.

One of the topics we discussed at a local steakhouse that afternoon was what Tony would remember the most about that championship season. It's one of those questions journalists ask simply because the answer often provides a foundation from which to build the article. Tony, however, didn't bite.

There wasn't one thing, he said. There always would be, he said, particular moments and particular people.

The observation wasn't revelatory, but it has remained with me. Why should someone attempt to reduce an achievement such as a national championship to one memory?

Thirty-five years later, Clemson celebrates another national championship, and *Clemson Crowned* won't attempt to limit you; instead, it will allow you to savor and to recall any number of particular moments and particular people.

All the moments are here. Some in particular will stir your memory simply by naming the opponent.

Auburn. Louisville. N.C. State. Florida State. *Pittsburgh.* South Carolina. Ohio State. ALABAMA.

And particular people are here, some like Deshaun Watson who won't ever be forgotten and some who years from now might not be so easy to remember.

Because of the efforts of reporters Scott Keepfer, Brad Senkiw, Manie Robinson and Dan Hope and of photographers Bart Boatwright and Ken Ruinard, you'll forever have those moments and people no more than a few page flips away.

As I'm sure it is with you, I already have my particular memories of the 2016 season. As one of those lucky enough to have witnessed two Clemson national championships, there are memories that link one title to the other: a particular catch by Perry Tuttle and one by Mike Williams; a fourth-quarter sack at Florida State and a fourth-quarter stop against Alabama.

But there's one particular link for me: Jay Guillermo, the starting center on the 2016 national champion team, weighs 310 pounds – 94 pounds *more* than the starting center on the 1981 national champion team.

Jim Rice
Sports Editor

Clemson quarterback Deshaun Watson scores on an 8-yard carry against Alabama during the second quarter of the national championship game. Watson led the Tigers' come-back victory and was named offensive MVP of the game. (Bart Boatwright/The Greenville News)

COLLEGE FOOTBALL PLAYOFF NATIONAL CHAMPIONSHIP

CLEMSON 35, ALABAMA 31
January 9, 2017 • Tampa, Florida

Clemson Fulfills Legacies, Wins National Title

Watson Brings Team Back from the Brink with Huge Play

By Brad Senkiw

elcome back, "Title Tigers." Welcome to immortality, Dabo Swinney and Deshaun Watson. And welcome to the 2016 national championship.

History was made, legacies fulfilled and a trophy hoisted by Clemson for the first time in 35 years as the Tigers knocked off vaunted Alabama 35-31 on Monday night at Raymond James Stadium when Watson found Hunter Renfrow for a 2-yard touchdown pass with one second remaining.

"Eight years ago, our goal was to work our tails off and eventually get Clemson back on top," said Swinney, who joined Danny Ford as the only Clemson coaches to capture national titles. "Tonight, that's a reality. It truly is. The paw is flying on top of the mountain tonight."

Clemson said all week it had to beat the best to be the best. Alabama, which had won four national titles since 2009, certainly represented that. After coming up five points short a year ago, a revenge game for Clemson didn't go the Tigers' way for over three quarters. They trailed for more than 45 minutes.

"We expected to win the game. We expected to win last year," Swinney said. "When we take the field, we expect to win."

And their championship drought ended at the hands of Watson.

"I couldn't have drawn up this scenario," said Watson, who announced he'll turn pro. "It is a blessing that we won this game tonight. I feel fortunate to have been part of this team. This was for all our fans tonight."

The drive that turned the game around for Clemson began with 6:33 left in the game. Mike Williams made a leaping 26-yard grab, and with an unsportsmanlike penalty tacked on, Clemson had first-and-10 at the 16. Watson got it down to the 1-yard line on the next snap, and Gallman scored on a dive into the end zone to give Clemson its first lead of the game at 24-21.

It didn't last long, though. Alabama went 68 yards in six plays and regained the lead on a 30-yard TD run by Tide quarterback Jalen Hurts, but the favored team left 2:07 on the clock.

"We're built for times like this," Watson said. "Let's go finish."

Watson went to work and moved the chains with a 24-yard pass to Williams and a 17-yard toss to Jordan

Deshaun Watson leaps over Alabama defensive back Ronnie Harrison to get to the 1-yard line during the fourth quarter. Watson ran for 43 yards during the game. (Bart Boatwright/The Greenville News)

Leggett that got Clemson first-and-goal at the Alabama 9 with 14 seconds to play. A pass interference call put the ball at the 2 with six seconds left.

Watson then took a snap, rolled to his right and there was Renfrow, wide open and sure-handed.

"Just an unbelievable play by Deshaun," Renfrow said. "Artavis Scott did a great job on the outside getting a little rub, and it was an awesome play call by our coaches."

It was a much tougher game for Watson than a year ago, when he amassed 478 total yards and four touchdowns, but it was an even better performance. That big, strong Alabama D-line totaled four sacks and pushed the Tigers' big boys up front around much of the night, but Watson did get enough clean pockets to make some plays.

Watson finished 36-of-56 passing for 420 yards through the air and another 43 yards on the ground. He threw for three TDs with no interceptions and ran for one more score.

Opposite: Clemson wide receiver Mike Williams catches a fourth-quarter touchdown past Alabama defensive back Marlon Humphrey. (Bart Boatwright/The Greenville News) Above: Dabo Swinney and the Tigers get ready for the rematch before their championship game against the Crimson Tide in Tampa. (Bart Boatwright/The Greenville News)

"It's my time to go (pro)," said Watson, who already has his degree. "Moments like this I'll never forget. Clemson was the best three years of my life."

Renfrow had 92 yards on 10 catches to go with his historic TD. Williams chipped in with eight receptions, 94 yards and a score. Deon Cain added 94 yards on five catches off the bench to help the offense total 511 yards against the best defense in the country.

The Clemson defense rebounded from a rough start and more than held its own against Alabama's physical running game. The Crimson Tide's one-dimensional offense was 2-for-15 on third downs.

After giving up 143 yards via the ground in the first half, the Tigers kept the Tide under 80 in the second half. It hurt Alabama when Bo Scarbrough, who had 93 yards and two touchdowns, left the game in the third quarter with a leg injury.

"We always miss a guy that's Bo Scarbrough, especially when you want to run the ball and take some time off the clock," Alabama coach Nick Saban said.

Opposite: Hunter Renfrow beats Alabama defensive back Tony Brown to catch the winning touchdown in the final seconds of the game, an unforgettable moment in Clemson football history. (Bart Boatwright/The Greenville News) Above: Clemson students witnessed the team's first national title since 1981. (Bart Boatwright/The Greenville News)

Alabama built a 14-0 lead early behind touchdown runs of 25 and 37 yards from Scarbrough. The Tigers finally got on the board on an 8-yard TD run by Watson at the 6:09 mark of the second quarter.

The next points scored didn't come until a 27-yard field goal by Alabama's Adam Griffith early in third quarter that put the Tide up 10.

The Tigers wouldn't go away. They scored on a 27-yard touchdown pass from Watson to Renfrow with 7:10 left in the third to cut the lead to 17-14. And after Alabama came right back with a 68-yard touchdown pass from Hurts to tight end O.J. Howard, Clemson answered with a 9-play, 72-yard drive that ended with a 4-yard TD pass from Watson to Williams that cut the lead to 24-21 with 14:00 to play in the game to set up the late-game dramatics.

"I just am so proud of these players," Swinney said.

Opposite: Clemson defensive lineman Dexter Lawrence (90), top, and defensive tackle Carlos Watkins (94) bring down Alabama running back Bo Scarbrough during the first quarter. Scarbrough had an effective game, with 93 yards and two touchdowns before leaving with an injury. (Bart Boatwright/The Greenville News) Above: Hunter Renfrow catches a touchdown in the third quarter, one of two scores on his big night in which he finished with 10 catches for 92 yards. (Bart Boatwright/ The Greenville News)

Clemson's path to history didn't come easy. The Tigers played eight games, including the last one, that were decided by a touchdown or less. N.C. State missed a field goal that would've beaten Clemson. Pitt dealt the Tigers their only loss of the season, but the hopes and dreams of a title didn't end.

"I can't tell you how humbled, how blessed I am to be a part of getting Clemson back on top," Swinney said. This moment, 35 years and doing something that a lot of people didn't think that we could do."

It only made Clemson hungrier and more focused, and after edging Virginia Tech to capture its second consecutive ACC title and dominating Ohio State 31-0 in the College Football Playoff's Fiesta Bowl, it all came down to one game, one moment and one Watson touchdown.

"Clemson waited 35 long years. It's finally coming home," Boulware said. "It's coming home!" ■

Opposite: Mike Williams goes high to pull down a pass in the fourth quarter. Williams made several clutch catches, finishing with eight for 94 yards and a touchdown. (Bart Boatwright/The Greenville News) Above: Clemson linebacker Ben Boulware kisses the national championship trophy after the Tigers rallied against Alabama. Boulware had six tackles, including two tackles for loss, and was exuberant during postgame celebrations. (Bart Boatwright/The Greenville News)

Deshaun Watson scores on an 8-yard carry in the second quarter. Clemson was down 14-0 at the time but the 87-yard scoring drive put them right back in the game. (Bart Boatwright/The Greenville News)

Watson Rises to the Occasion and Brings Title to Clemson

First National Title Since 1981 Is Sweet for the Tigers

By Dan Hope

In his final act as Clemson's starting quarterback, Deshaun Watson cemented his legacy as the greatest football player in school history.

Watson completed 36 of 56 passing attempts for 420 yards and three touchdowns and ran for 43 yards and another touchdown to lead the Tigers to a 35-31 win over Alabama and Clemson's second national championship.

The Clemson quarterback wasn't great for the entire game – he completed 13 of 23 passes for 153 yards and rushed for only one yard in the first half – but when the game was on the line, Watson was at his best.

Watson completed nine of his final 10 passing attempts, including the game-winning, 2-yard touchdown to Hunter Renfrow with only one second left in the game.

He completed at least three passes to six different receivers, while he engineered four touchdown drives for the Tigers that were longer than 68 yards.

"Maybe now everybody will understand when I tell them Deshaun Watson's the best player in the country," Clemson coach Dabo Swinney said after the game. "He showed it again tonight on the biggest stage."

Watson's one major flaw over the course of the season was throwing 17 interceptions, but he didn't throw any in the biggest game of the year. His only turnover against Alabama came when he was unable to handle an inaccurate shotgun snap by center Jay Guillermo.

His 420 passing yards was his second-highest total of the season, while his three passing touchdowns and four total touchdowns tied his season-highs.

Watson accounted for all but 48 of Clemson's offensive yards in the game, and became the first Heisman runner-up quarterback to win the national championship since 2005.

This wasn't the first time Watson had a great national championship game performance against Alabama. He threw for 405 yards and four touchdowns and rushed for 73 yards against the Crimson Tide in last year's title game. This time, though, the Tigers came out on top.

Being interviewed by ESPN minutes after the game was over, the Gainesville, Georgia, product could hardly put what he had just accomplished into words.

"I'm speechless," Watson said. "It's not just for me. It's for all the alumni, the fans, my city in Gainesville,

Deshaun Watson went out on top at Clemson, leading the Tigers to a national championship and definitively claiming his status as the best player in program history. (Bart Boatwright/The Greenville News)

my family. It's bigger than just me. This just impacts so many people across the world."

Watson, who graduated from Clemson in December and is projected to be one of the top picks in the 2017 NFL draft, finished his Tigers career with more than 10,000 passing yards, nearly 2,000 rushing yards and 116 total touchdowns. His game-winning touchdown pass, his 41st scoring toss of the year, set the ACC single-season record for touchdown passes.

The two-time Heisman finalist's Clemson career is over, but his accomplishments – none bigger than the national title – ensure he won't soon be forgotten.

Watson said winning the national title was a moment he will never forget.

"Clemson was the best three years of my life," Watson said. ■

Opposite: Deshaun Watson took some time to find his footing against Alabama with an average first half performance, but then stepped up in the key moments down the stretch and made Clemson football history. (Bart Boatwright/The Greenville News) Above: Clemson linebacker Ben Boulware hugs quarterback Deshaun Watson after the monumental win. On a Clemson team for the ages, Boulware and Watson will always stand out among the best players and most memorable personalities. (Bart Boatwright/The Greenville News)

Can Cornhole Keep Clemson Sharp?

Dabo Swinney uses Cornhole to Break Up the Monotony of August Camp

By Mandrallius Robinson • August 10, 2016

The team formed a circle in the middle of the practice field. Two players lined up on opposite ends. They exchanged glares. It had the intensity of an Oklahoma drill, with slightly less contact.

It was a game of cornhole.

The popular beanbag toss variant of horseshoes is a staple of tailgates and backyard barbeques. It normally does not generate the passion it has produced during recent Clemson University football practices.

Clemson coach Dabo Swinney turned cornhole from a lighthearted pastime to a motivational tool. He simply raised the stakes.

Clemson's sprawling practice facilities require players to traverse across fields between periods. In Swinney's cornhole tournament, players competed for the privilege to remain on one field throughout the entire practice. It may seem like a small wager, but, under the pressure of an unrelenting practice regimen and the remorseless August sun, any amount of relief is welcomed. The option to shed about 200 yards of jogging off the workload is worth a toss.

On Monday, Swinney playfully critiqued his players' cornhole skills.

"It's been back and forth. We can't seem to get a consistent winner," Swinney said. "Hopefully, in their spare time they'll compete and work on that. Gotta coach 'em up."

Pulling out those wooden boards is a delightful diversion amid the monotonous drudge of August camp. Yet, Swinney hopes it also will reinforce the competitive edge Clemson's lofty goals demand. The tactic fits Swinney, who admittedly is as charged for Family Game Night as he is for the College Football Playoff. His competitive juices are always flowing, but through camp, his players may require an occasional squeeze.

Of course, cornhole is not a definitive indicator of intensity or effectiveness. That arm motion is not going to help a quarterback's touch on third down. It certainly will not assist any tackles. The defense won the cornhole challenge after the stretch period Monday. Yet, on the first play of an ensuing intra-squad scrimmage, it allowed a 99-yard touchdown run.

Swinney was less playful in his critique of that effort.

Nevertheless, Swinney's strategy is shrewd. Through the next six months, the diversions cannot be distractions. The otherwise innocent details require sharp focus, to preserve the team's goals and protect against complacency. For a program in Clemson's position, mental clarity is just as important as muscle dexterity.

Junior quarterback Deshaun Watson is a Heisman Trophy favorite who has graced the cover of recent editions of *Sports Illustrated* and *ESPN The Magazine.* Clemson was voted No. 2 in the Amway *USA TODAY* Sports preseason

Clemson players shake up their training camp routine with a game of cornhole during practice.
(Bart Boatwright/The Greenville News)

coaches poll. The Tigers are expected to end their 10-year losing streak in Tallahassee against Florida State, repeat as Atlantic Coast Conference champions and return to the National Championship Game.

Clemson never has entered a season with such expectations. The preseason chatter is tempting because it has never been this flattering. If you let widespread conjecture tell it, the Tigers already have reached Tampa. Swinney, his staff and most of his players understand

that they have not even reached September. They must be reminded that most of the people talking know very little about what is required to back it up.

Whether it is a toss of a beanbag or an extra period of first-team scrimmages, Clemson must pour all of its competitive juice into its preparation. That can be draining. Thus, Swinney must determine how to replenish the supply and ensure the Tigers will still have enough flowing when the real competition begins. ■

CLEMSON 19, AUBURN 13
September 3, 2016 • Auburn, Alabama

Clemson Beats Auburn to Start Season Off Right

Offense Wasn't Running on All Cylinders for First Game of the Season

By Scott Keepfer

O K, so Saturday night's – er, Sunday morning's – 19-13 victory against Auburn didn't exactly provide the type of offensive fireworks many Clemson fans expected.

Clemson was held to its lowest point total in 20 games dating back to the 2014 season, and the Tigers failed to post at least 500 yards of offense for the first time in 11 games.

But it wasn't a total washout, either.

Clemson coach Dabo Swinney said Sunday evening that after viewing the game video he was encouraged by several realizations, including:

• **The offense had its opportunities.** "We had four drops, including three touchdowns," Swinney said. That included two drops by Mike Williams that should have been easy scores.

"He obviously made some huge plays, but there are more than just stats at that position," Swinney said. "He graded about 78 percent, and that's not a winning grade for a wideout. It was his first game in a year, and he did some good stuff, but we've got to get him better."

• **Auburn's defense was pretty good.** Swinney will feel better if Auburn's defense continues to flex its muscle. "We had some missed plays we didn't finish and weren't as sharp as we want to be, but give Auburn some credit," Swinney said. "They were pretty doggone good defensively."

Auburn appeared to have several future NFL players on defense, including defensive tackle Montravius Adams, end Carl Lawson and linebacker Deshaun Davis; that unit may help Auburn make some noise in the SEC.

• **The offensive line allowed no sacks.** First-time starter Taylor Hearn blended with the unit impressively at left guard and was named the team's offensive player of the game.

"He did a really good job," Swinney said. "I'm really proud of Taylor."

• **The offense came up big in crunch time.** "To take that ball with 3:20 left after they've just scored and have momentum, and we march down the field – that was huge," Swinney said. "It was good to see our guys respond

Wide receiver Hunter Renfrow catches a crucial touchdown pass during the fourth quarter of Clemson's season-opening nail biter. (Ken Ruinard/Independent Mail)

and show some maturity in that situation. That was the sign of an experienced football team with a lot of poise."

Behind Wayne Gallman and Deshaun Watson, Clemson drove 60 yards in 10 plays to take 2:42 off the clock, allowing Auburn only 40 seconds to drive 83 yards. Gallman carried six times for 34 yards on the drive.

TOP PLAYERS

While Hearn was named offensive player of the game, the defensive honor went to sophomore Christian Wilkins who was making his first start at defensive end. Wilkins had six tackles, including 2.5 tackles for loss and one sack. He also had a fumble recovery, broke up a pass and was credited with a quarterback hurry.

Holder Seth Ryan was named special teams player of the game after plucking a high snap out of the air and placing it quickly on a 40-yard Greg Huegel field goal in the third quarter. ■

Opposite: Running back Wayne Gallman drives down the field in the closing minutes of Clemson's 19-13 victory. (Ken Ruinard/Independent Mail) Above: Cornerback Cordrea Tankersley (left) reacts during the first half of his team's clash with Auburn. (Getty Images)

Dexter Lawrence Debuts

Defense Locked and Loaded for Winning Season

By Mandrallius Robinson • September 5, 2016

The advertisements were frequent but brief. They were intriguing but indefinite. They were more teasers than trailers.

We heard hints of praise from Clemson University coaches. We heard intimations of marvel from teammates.

The advertisements did not do the story justice.

Dexter Lawrence is far better than advertised.

We could simply look on the roster and infer that a 6-foot-5, 340-pound freshman defensive tackle would be imposing. We could watch him strolling through stretches before his first practice and observe that he was uniquely nimble.

We could assume he would contribute early and disrupt often.

However, until we could see him swat away blockers like mosquitos at a cookout, until we could see him chase down a quarterback with the agility of an outside linebacker, until we could see him for ourselves, we could not know that the praise and marvel was never exaggerated.

Lawrence's premiere at Auburn University on Saturday night was pure spectacle. He commanded attention at a usually thankless position. He starred in the latest installment of the running series of blockbusters titled "Clemson's defensive line."

Clemson lost its starting defensive ends from last season, Shaq Lawson and Kevin Dodd, to the National Football League. Projected replacement Austin Bryant suffered a foot injury in preseason camp and missed Saturday's opener.

To compensate, Clemson shifted Lawrence's fellow phenomenon Christian Wilkins from tackle to end. Yet, Clemson still had enough depth in the interior, with senior Carlos Watkins and junior Scott Pagano, that Lawrence was not even in the starting lineup.

However, on his first snap, Lawrence's power was captivating. He penetrated the line so easily, he surprised himself.

"When the offensive lineman came down on me, I kind of stood him up. I was like, 'OK, I've been blocked harder than this,'" Lawrence said. "I just tried to embrace the moment as much as I could."

With the seasoning of experience and expertise, Lawrence could emerge as a dominant disruptive force. He recorded five tackles and a sack in the first half alone.

"I'm a little upset, because he got the first sack of the season. I really wanted that," teased Wilkins, who registered a sack on the next down.

Lawrence and Wilkins finished the game with 13 total tackles. They even lined up together in the jumbo package on offense and cleared a four-lane highway to the end zone for running back Wayne Gallman.

"They kind of hopped out of the way," Wilkins said of the wise defenders. "We didn't have to do much, but I'm glad we got the score.

"That was fun. I like that. Maybe we'll put down a couple more plays in that package."

Clemson's front controlled the line of scrimmage. Auburn netted four yards on its first seven rushes. By halftime, that rushing total was reduced to a single yard. Auburn closed with 87 rushing yards.

Auburn running back Kerryon Johnson exploited a few cracks in the defense and rushed for 94 yards on

Freshman defensive lineman Dexter Lawrence lived up to expectations in his debut against Auburn. (Bart Boatwright/The Greenville News)

23 carries, including a 9-yard touchdown. Yet, no other Auburn rusher averaged more than 1.8 yards per carry.

Behind the defensive line, Clemson revealed a refortified linebacker corps, anchored by the return of Ben Boulware. Kendall Joseph filled the void left by leading tackler B.J. Goodson. He led Clemson with nine stops.

The secondary was not stressed often by Auburn's inept passing attack. With the exception of a 43-yard pass in the fourth quarter, Clemson grounded Auburn's offense for 14 completions on 29 attempts for 132 yards. Clemson receiver Mike Williams gained more receiving yards (174) by himself.

Clemson recorded two interceptions and five pass breakups, including Jadar Johnson's victory-sealing swat on the final play of the game.

Auburn notched two third-down conversions during a field goal drive in the first half. Clemson spoiled Auburn's next 11 third-down plays.

"It just shows that we have the potential to be a really good defense this year," Wilkins said. "We were confident all along. We knew it didn't matter who we put out there. We were going to go as hard as we can."

Auburn's three-man quarterback shuffle interrupted its offensive rhythm. Its ineffectiveness aided Clemson's reloaded defense. There certainly are more prolific offenses awaiting on the schedule.

Yet, Saturday night's performance is an advertisement to any detractors. Clemson's defense has not lost its luster.

This time, the message will not be confined to conjecture. Before the next 11 showings, we will know about the coming attraction. ■

CLEMSON 30, TROY 24
September 10, 2016 • Clemson, South Carolina

Clemson Overcomes Struggling Offense to Beat Troy

No. 2 Tigers Hold Off Troy in Home Opener after Enduring Another Out-Of-Sync Game

By Brad Senkiw

arly in the fourth quarter, standing at the Troy 1-yard line and facing third down, Clemson QB Deshaun Watson dropped back and tossed a touchdown pass to… Christian Wilkins?

That sounds like a play that the No. 2 Tigers might run in an easy rout over the visitors from the Sun Belt, or maybe save for a tight ACC contest.

But no, Clemson needed to pull out an unconventional scoring play to a defensive lineman just to get some breathing room from the Trojans in the final quarter of the Tigers' Saturday's 30-24 victory over Troy in front of 78,532 fans at Memorial Stadium.

That play, which Clemson head coach Dabo Swinney was happy about because a Tiger caught the ball, showed what kind of game the offense was playing in the home opener.

"I thought (Troy) played well enough to win today," Clemson head coach Dabo Swinney said. "I thought we played bad enough to lose in a lot of areas. But at the end of the day, it's all about winning and finding a way to get it done, and we certainly did that."

A week after getting by with a 19-13 win at Auburn, where Clemson didn't look like the high-scoring, dominating College Football Playoff contender it expects

to be, the Tigers were still suffering from a lack of execution against a team they were supposed to pound by five touchdowns.

It took three consecutive scoring drives and 17 points in the fourth quarter to thwart the Trojans' upset attempt. On a day where the offense racked up more than 400 yards, it could've been much, much more as drops, overthrows and three turnovers defined a win that still helped Clemson move to 2-0.

"The biggest disappointment today was offense," Swinney said. "We had 414 yards of offense, and I don't know if we can play worse to be honest with you. It's very frustrating because we're a rhythm offense and we're not making the routine plays. If we don't do that, it disrupts the rhythm of everything."

Watson needed 53 passing attempts, a career-high, to reach 292 yards. He also threw two interceptions and missed on several deep balls, but Watson did connect on a trio of touchdown passes.

"We all made some mistakes, had some missed opportunities, but it's on to the next play," Watson said. "It happens sometimes. It's life. It's football. No one's perfect."

He also had to lead the running game with 55 rushing yards. Wayne Gallman, who had 30 for 123

Wide receiver Trevion Thompson drops a fourth-quarter pass in what was an arduous game for the Tigers' offense. (Bart Boatwright/The Greenville News)

yards at Auburn, had just 34 yards on nine carries.

The receivers did little to get the offense going, and Ray-Ray McCloud gave Troy a gift in the second quarter when he dropped the ball at the 1-yard line while walking into the end zone on a 75-yard punt return.

"We're not playing to our potential on offense right now. That's frustrating for all of us," Clemson co-offensive coordinator Jeff Scott said. "We're not clicking the way that we know that we can. We know what we have in that room. For whatever reason we're just not on the right page right now, but we'll get that right."

The Tigers got off to a sluggish start as the offensive line struggled early and collected a couple penalties, players began to press, and little went right in the first three quarters. They were tied 3-3 in the second quarter until Watson found Hunter Renfrow for a 35-yard TD grab. But Troy answered with a 66-yard TD run by Jabir Frye, and Greg Huegel, who made three field goals on the day, made a 32-yarder with 2:45 left in the half just to give Clemson a 13-10 halftime lead.

"Today's performance was not acceptable, not up to our standard," co-offensive coordinator Tony Elliott said.

Nobody got on the scoreboard in the third quarter, and it wasn't until Watson found Wilkins that the Tiger faithful began showing signs of relaxing.

After a 23-yard TD pass from Watson to Deon Cain, who had a few drops himself, with 10 minutes to play, Troy (1-1) had a couple of calls not go its way, but the Trojans didn't go away. QB Brandon Silvers hooked up with Deondre Douglas for two fourth-quarter TD passes against a Clemson defense that gave up 386 total yards.

"They honestly in some ways, in some aspects, outplayed us," Wilkins said. "They really fought hard."

The Tigers, who did force three turnovers, took the positive of victory away from Saturday, but the road back to the playoff is going to be much tougher down the road. And Swinney doesn't believe there's anything major wrong with his squad. It was not doing the "little things" that lead to "big things" that frustrated him the most.

"I'm never going to apologize for a win," Swinney said. "I'm never going to be the guy that doesn't appreciate a win."

However, he "expects guys to make the plays that are there. That's a reflection of us as coaches." ∎

Just shy of the end zone, wide receiver Ray-Ray McCloud drops the ball on what should have been a 75-yard punt return for a touchdown in the second quarter. Clemson just managed to grind out a win over Troy in front of the Memorial Stadium crowd. (Bart Boatwright/The Greenville News)

#10 LINEBACKER
BEN BOULWARE

Former T.L. Hanna Product Sets the Pace for Defense

By Dan Hope • July 25, 2016

Being successful in football is as much about desire and work ethic as it is about physical ability.

That's what's enabled Ben Boulware to become the face of the Clemson defense going into his senior year.

A four-star recruit out of T.L. Hanna High School in 2012, Boulware began his career as a role player. He played mostly on special teams (just 73 defensive snaps) as a freshman, then came off the bench for most of his sophomore year. But after a productive junior season, in which he started all 15 games and earned All-ACC honors, Boulware is Clemson's leading returning tackler and expected to be the linchpin of its linebacker corps.

There are other linebackers who are taller and other linebackers who are faster, but on a defense that needs senior leadership, 'no one's more invested' than Boulware, said Clemson defensive coordinator Brent Venables.

"He cares a great deal about the team and about our performance day in and day out," Venables said. "He knows how to work and loves the grind."

Leading the Way

Some leaders lead by example, while others lead vocally.

Boulware does both.

On the field, Boulware is known for giving maximum effort. Even during the final four games of last season, when Boulware was battling a shoulder injury, he could be seen making plays all over the field.

"He is just relentless to get his job done," said Clemson coach Dabo Swinney. "He's relentless to get the football. It's hard to coach that in guys. And that's just in his DNA.

"He's just one of those guys that ain't going to go away. He's a long day's work for the opponent, because he's going to keep coming."

Venables described Boulware as "one of those few guys on the front line that can survive World War I, World War II and World War III." Kenya Fouch, who coached Boulware at T.L. Hanna, described his former player as a "Tasmanian devil."

"The whole time he was at Hanna, I tried to get

Ben Boulware celebrates after Clemson stopped Auburn on fourth down in the season opener. (Bart Boatwright/The Greenville News)

him to slow down," Fouch said. "Coach Venables has done a great job of getting him to see things happening in front of him, and that has really allowed him to make a lot more plays."

Both Fouch and Venables describe Boulware as someone who is always at the "front of the line." Because of that, he has earned the respect of his teammates. Boulware has been known to demand additional work during conditioning drills, both at T.L. Hanna and at Clemson, and his teammates have followed his lead.

"Whatever the coaches' idea for conditioning was, it was never enough for Ben," Fouch said. "Even on a day where we felt like we absolutely killed them, he always wanted to do more and I can't ever remember a time when a player refused his request. If Ben said 'Hey, we're going to do more,' then everybody stayed and did more. But you can have that authority when everybody knows that you're in the front of the line, that you've been working hardest of everybody.'

Swinney describes Boulware as "one of those guys that you just can't help but gravitate to."

"He's a loud leader. He's loud about how he plays; he's loud just by how he leads," Swinney said. "He's got a great personality. He's funny. He is intense. And he hates to lose. It doesn't matter if it's a drill in practice, whatever. He hates to lose."

Boulware is set to be Clemson's starting weakside linebacker in 2016, and is one of only three returning starters on the Tigers defense, all seniors, along with defensive tackle Carlos Watkins and cornerback Cordrea Tankersley.

Growing up

Boulware, it seems now, is everything a coach would want in a player.

In addition to his work with the football team, Boulware is a two-time All-ACC Academic selection. The Anderson native is just 10 credit hours away from graduating with a degree in sociology.

"It's crazy, because I remember getting to Clemson and it's like 'God, these four years are going to take so long,' but it went by so quick," Boulware said.

Boulware admits, though, that he still had some growing up to do when he got to Clemson.

"Coming into this program, I was very selfish," Boulware said. "I think a lot of athletes coming into top programs, you come in highly recruited, you think you're going to come in and start, be a freshman All-American, this and that. In most cases that's not how it is."

During his sophomore year, Boulware questioned whether Clemson was right for him, whether it was the place he wanted to be. He credits his coaches and his veteran teammates at the time, including current New Orleans Saints linebacker Stephone Anthony, with getting him refocused and to where he is now.

"I think being around such great leadership at Clemson, with Coach Swinney, Coach Venables and all the great players we've had here, it's easy to go through that maturation process, because we have so much help around us," Boulware said.

Swinney said Boulware is "one of those guys we have to sometimes kind of channel the right way," but the coach is proud of how his player has grown in his collegiate career.

"He's definitely become a great leader for us over his three years here," Swinney said.

Getting better

Going into his senior year, Boulware is still working on getting better. Specifically, Boulware has focused this offseason on losing weight. After playing at 245 pounds most of last season, and at 248 pounds in the national championship game, Boulware wants to be between 235 to 238 pounds this season.

Boulware, who says he was recently timed at 4.61 seconds in the 40-yard dash, expects to be faster on the field as a result.

"I think (playing at 245 pounds) helped me out a

One of three returning seniors on the Tigers' roster, Ben Boulware is an undeniable team leader with his constant preparedness and drive to improve. (Bart Boatwright/The Greenville News)

lot in the box, being able to just be explosive and hold my own, but I think it also hurt me when I was outside the box, trying to make plays out in the open, because I was too heavy," Boulware said. "If I'm trying to guard a tight end or a running back in the open, I got to lose weight to be able to stay with them."

Boulware made headlines this offseason when he responded on Twitter to a critique from NFL draft analyst Jon Ledyard that described his athleticism as "limited." So it shouldn't come as a surprise that Boulware is seeking to improve upon his athleticism.

"I love coaching players that have a chip on their shoulder when people have doubted them," Venables said. "Everybody wants to talk about on the outside looking in what he can't do. Ben takes it personal. He's got an edge to him."

Swinney believes Boulware is comparable to Luke Kuechly, a three-time All-Pro linebacker for the NFL's Carolina Panthers, in that both of them "play faster than they are because of their anticipation."

"He's faster than people think," Swinney said of Boulware. "He really runs pretty well. He can move. But he's just so smart. He studies the game."

Boulware admits he might not be the most impressive physical specimen, but he believes his performance on the field demonstrates his ability.

"I'm definitely not the biggest or the fastest, but I make plays, and that's just not me being cocky, that's just you can watch the film and the film speaks for itself," Boulware said this spring.

Over his first three years at Clemson, Boulware has better learned how to prepare for each game, and that has made him a better player, Venables said.

"I think he'll be the first to admit his first year that it's like 'I got this, I'll just do what I did' and just go find a guy with the ball," Venables said. "He had to grow up, learning how to prepare and then the willingness to consistently invest and to do the little things. He found that secret sauce, he liked it and he can't get enough of it."

Boulware, who says he prepares the same way for every game regardless of the opponent, believes that preparation is the key to his success.

"When I go into a game, I'm not stressed at all. I'm not nervous or scared of anything, just because I'm so prepared going into each game," Boulware said. ■

Ben Boulware shows off his ability to quickly anticipate and react, knocking the ball loose from South Carolina quarterback Brandon McIlwain. (Ken Ruinard/Independent Mail)

CLEMSON 59, SOUTH CAROLINA STATE 0
September 17, 2016 • Clemson, South Carolina

Tigers Steamroll Past S.C. State

Clean Game Just What the Doctor Ordered for Clemson

By Scott Keepfer

Clemson, which had plenty of drops in its first two games, had another on Saturday.

The Tigers dropped a bomb on South Carolina State.

Clemson posted a school-record 31 first-quarter points and rolled to a 59-0 victory against the out-manned Bulldogs in front of 79,590 at Memorial Stadium.

How lopsided was it?

• Clemson played three quarterbacks – in the *first* quarter.

• A record 15 different players caught a pass and a record five quarterbacks had a completion.

• Both coaches agreed to shorten the final two quarters from 15 to 12 minutes, which offered at least some relief to the visiting Bulldogs, who managed only nine first downs.

For Clemson, it was just what the doctor ordered for a team whose offense had left plenty to be desired in uncomfortably close victories against Auburn and Troy in the season's first two weeks.

"I'm proud of our guys," Clemson coach Dabo Swinney said. "They played a clean game for four quarters. It was great for our team, our spirit and our morale."

The fact that the morale boost came against a winless S.C. State (0-3) team seemed inconsequential; the Tigers were in dire need of a "clean" game regardless of the talent level of the opposition, and they got just that while injecting a shot of confidence into the vast majority of the 92 players who saw the field.

"They were dialed in, very crisp," Swinney said. "It was a game that we should dominate, and we did."

Clemson, which was ranked No. 3 in the latest Amway Coaches Poll, extended its school-record home winning streak to 18 consecutive games. The Tigers haven't lost at Memorial Stadium since a 51-14 loss to Florida State on Oct. 19, 2013.

Clemson improved to 31-0 against FCS opponents, and has won 30 of the 31 games by double digits.

Quarterback Deshaun Watson, who apologized to the media on Monday for emitting a "negative energy," gave off quite the positive vibe on Saturday, bouncing back with a coolly efficient 12 of 15 effort for 152 yards and three touchdowns in barely a quarter's worth of playing time.

It also was big bounce-back game for sophomore wide receiver Ray Ray McCloud, who was just one week removed a major gaffe that turned a 75-yard punt return for a touchdown into a 74-yard gain and fumble at the 1-yard line.

Clemson defensive back Jadar Johnson returns an interception against an overmatched South Carolina State team. (Bart Boatwright/The Greenville News)

"I always have a chip on my shoulder, but I just showed myself a little more today," McCloud said. "On special teams I wanted to make a difference and put last week behind me."

McCloud did just that to the tune of 116 all-purpose yards, including a pair of touchdown receptions, and three punt returns for 56 yards.

The defense pitched a shutout, holding S.C. State to 102 total yards while registering 10 tackles for loss, including five sacks.

"We knew what we had, we just had to fix what was inside us," linebacker Jalen Williams said. "We know what we've got."

While McCloud was busy burying his past and Williams busy extracting maximum effort, the Tigers quickly and collectively began turning their focus toward the future, which begins in short order with a Thursday night game at Georgia Tech in their Atlantic Coast Conference opener.

The Tigers then host red-hot Louisville on Oct. 1.

When asked what he thought about Louisville's 63-20 thrashing of Florida State on Saturday, Williams pleaded the fifth.

"Get ready for GT (Georgia Tech)," Williams said. "That's all I have to say about that."

Forrest Gump notwithstanding, that should be music to Swinney's ears.

The Tigers haven't won at Georgia Tech in Atlanta since 2003, which is more than enough reason to place a showdown against Louisville on Oct. 1 on the back burner for at least another five days.

In the meantime, the Tigers were finally feeling fat and happy Saturday afternoon, and few could argue their status.

Three games.

Three victories.

No negative energy.

"We're confident," Williams said. "Why wouldn't we be? We're 3-0." ■

Running back Wayne Gallman has the end zone in his sights during Clemson's 59-0 win. (Bart Boatwright/The Greenville News)

Wilkins, Lawrence Embracing Roles in 'Jumbo Package'

Clemson Duo Ready to Get Season Started

By Scott Keepfer • September 9, 2016

hen your football team needs only a yard for a touchdown, it's not exactly rocket science.

"It's not like you're going to trick a lot of people," Clemson coach Dabo Swinney said.

Particularly when you line up a pair of burly defensive linemen in the backfield in what is commonly known as a "jumbo package."

Clemson employed the configuration Saturday against Auburn, with defensive behemoths Dexter Lawrence and Christian Wilkins assuming the roles of lead blockers for running back Wayne Gallman on a fourth-and-goal play midway through the second quarter.

The result? Gallman strolled into the end zone, untouched, in what he termed "the easiest thing I've ever done in college."

So is the usage of two defensive standouts who weigh in at a combined 650 pounds as road graders something Clemson fans can expect to see again?

"I'm hoping there's more in store," Wilkins said. "It's a shorter run for me to celebrate with someone when they get in the end zone instead of having to sprint all the way from the sidelines."

And who knows – perhaps Deshaun Watson will simply hand the ball off to Wilkins if the opportunity arises, rekindling memories of former Clemson great William "Refrigerator" Perry, who might be best remembered for his two career rushing touchdowns in the NFL than he was for his defensive prowess.

"I told the coaches every time I'm in we score a touchdown," said Wilkins, who caught a pass on a fake punt that led to a touchdown in the Tigers' Orange Bowl win against Oklahoma last year. "Maybe I can get in on some of that 'Fridge' action."

Swinney was non-committal on the future of the "jumbo package," but rest assured that the lineup is bound to surface again based on its successful debut; perhaps not Saturday against Troy, or the following week against S.C. State, but it certainly appears to be a viable and logical option when Atlantic Coast Conference action heats up.

"You never know," Swinney said. "We throw fake punts to defensive tackles."

The idea of going jumbo struck Swinney when he first saw the 6-foot-5, 340-pound Lawrence on campus last January as a mid-year enrollee.

"When we signed Dexter and I saw him, I thought, 'Yeah, we're going to be using this big boy,'" Swinney said. "I brought it to him this summer and we just started practicing it in fall camp.

"We can go to it when we need it. Most of the time the bigger, talented guy beats the smaller,

Defensive linemen Dexter Lawrence (left) and Christian Wilkins (right) have become a formidable duo on the Clemson squad. (Bart Boatwright/The Greenville News)

talented guy. And those are some big, heavy-duty guys who take pride in it."

That they do.

"It was fun," Lawrence said. "I told Wayne he was going to score no matter what.

"Nobody was in the hole (on the play). I just tried to blow something up and there was nothing there to blow up."

Co-offensive coordinator Tony Elliott directed all credit for the strategy to Swinney.

"That was Coach Swinney's deal," Elliott said. "We worked on it toward the end of camp and they took unbelievable pride in it. It's something that no one has seen us do, and it worked for us."

Wilkins, who at 6-4, 310 pounds is the smaller of the two goal-line blockers, said the approach is simplistic.

"Just run over the first person you see," he said.

That mission should be no trouble for Lawrence or Wilkins, who combined for 13 tackles, including 3½ tackles for loss, on the defensive side of the ball against Auburn.

If this keeps up, Wilkins could end up being a unique honoree.

"Who knows?" Wilkins said. "Maybe someday I can be Defensive Player of the Week and Offensive Player of the Week." ■

CLEMSON 26, GEORGIA TECH 7
September 22, 2016 • Atlanta, Georgia

Tigers End Losing Skid at Bobby Dodd Stadium

Win Moves Team to 4-0 Record

By Brad Senkiw

After two uneven performances in wins over Auburn and Troy to start the year, and a rout over a struggling FCS team last Saturday that proved very little, No. 3 Clemson faced its biggest challenge yet Thursday night at Georgia Tech, a house of horrors in recent years for the Tigers.

Despite not passing all of their tests with flying colors Thursday, they relied on a dominant defense against a triple-option attack and Deshaun Watson's first-half throwing prowess to beat Georgia Tech 26-7 in front of 53,932 fans at Bobby Dodd Stadium to earn their first win in Atlanta since 2003.

Ending that five-game streak and earning another victory is something they'll gladly take back to Death Valley.

"This is a place we hadn't won very much, so mission accomplished," said Clemson coach Dabo Swinney. "We're happy to get out of here with a 'W.' It's been a long time. I love the fight of our guys. I love the preparation. Hats off to Georgia Tech, but our guys were locked in."

Swinney said he was told after the game that it marked the first time since 1903 that Clemson came into this contest at Georgia Tech undefeated and left that way.

The offense built a 23-0 halftime lead behind a pair of Watson touchdown passes. The Tigers (4-0, 1-0 ACC) produced just three points in the second half, but getting a 13-year monkey off their backs on short rest looked easy for much of the night.

Clemson held Tech (3-1, 1-1) to 124 total yards and kept the Jackets off the scoreboard until the 13:21 mark of the fourth quarter.

Tech gained some momentum early in the fourth when it cut the lead to 23-7, but an interception on the next Yellow Jackets possession by Van Smith led to a 47-yard field goal and a 26-7 lead with 9:57 to play.

"I thought we were disciplined all night and just did our job," said Clemson defensive end Christian Wilkins. "No one was being selfish or trying to do somebody else's job or make this play or that play."

Clemson held Georgia Tech to 95 rushing yards. Quarterback Justin Thomas had just 29 passing yards and -25 yards rushing.

"It wasn't anything that we didn't see the first three weeks," said Thomas about Clemson's defense. "We've just got to come out and execute a little better and get prepared for the next opponent."

Swinney became the eighth coach in ACC history to win 50 conference games with the victory, and Clemson

With dozens of friends and family members there to watch him, Georgia native Deshaun Watson racked up 304 yards in his team's victory over Georgia Tech. (Bart Boatwright/The Greenville News)

improved its regular-season winning streak to 19 games.

"We came here to be 4-0, and that's what we got done," Swinney said. "We didn't win the division tonight, but we got off to a good start. We've got four wins, two of them on the road at tough places. That says a little bit about the toughness of our guys. I love that."

Watson threw for 262 of his 304 yards in the first half. He completed 32 of his 48 passes on the night. He tossed one interception but found receiver Ray-Ray McCloud eight times for 101 yards.

"(Watson) was our field general out there," said Clemson co-offensive coordinator Tony Elliott. "He did some things managing the game that we needed him to do. I thought he looked comfortable."

Elliott said Georgia Tech ran some soft coverages in the first half that he was anticipating. While the Yellow Jackets pressed more on the receivers in the second half, Clemson took advantage of that choice of coverage on receivers like McCloud early on.

In the first 30 minutes of the game, Clemson had 347 total yards to Georgia Tech's 22, and 16 more first downs.

"I thought it was good rhythm early on. We were able to put together some drives from the opening snaps," Elliott said. "We were able to build on that momentum that I think we started at the end of that Troy game and then last week. It was good to get off to a good start.

"We were clicking. We were spreading the ball around. Guys were playing fast. Tempo was looking good. I was really, really pleased with how the first half went."

The Tigers marched 75 yards on the first drive of the game in nine plays and went up 7-0 when Watson found Mike Williams for a 4-yard touchdown pass.

After a 27-yard missed field goal by Greg Huegel, the Tigers converted a third-and-long on an 18-yard pass to McCloud. Watson then found Trevion Thompson for a 25-yard gain inside the Tech 5-yard line,

and Gallman punched it in from the 1 for a 14-0 lead with 2:26 left in the first quarter.

Clemson added two more points to the scoreboard when Watson threw a pass that was intercepted in the Tech end zone by Lance Austin, but Austin fumbled the ball at the 2 and recovered it in the end zone for a safety.

"Very disappointed with our performance. It comes back to me," said Georgia Tech coach Paul Johnson. "I'll take credit for that. Offensively, the first (half) was embarrassing. That's ridiculous. They've got a good defensive football team, they've got some good players, but it didn't seem like we could get in their way."

The Tigers doubled up on the Yellow Jackets' mistake when they went 72 yards in less than two minutes and scored on a 9-yard touchdown pass from Watson to Jordan Leggett with four seconds left before halftime.

After running 56 plays in the first half, Clemson had just two series in the third quarter, and the game slowed down greatly. Tech came back stronger in the second half, but the Tigers were able to force a turnover on downs with 2:51 remaining in the game.

"We just wanted to run out the clock and get out of there with a 'W,'" said Watson, a Gainesville, Georgia, native who estimated he had 50 family and friends at the game. "There's little things that we can fix ... to make sure that we're all on the same page."

Gallman finished the game with 59 yards on 12 carries, and Watson added 36 yards on the ground. ■

Defensive tackle Carlos Watkins sacks Georgia Tech quarterback Justin Thomas during the first quarter at Bobby Dodd Stadium. (Bart Boatwright/The Greenville News)

Louisville's Lamar Jackson Could Ruin Clemson's Plans

Showdown Set for Death Valley

By Mandrallius Robinson • September 24, 2016

List the statistics University of Louisville quarterback Lamar Jackson has compiled through four games this season.

Tally the 13 touchdowns he has tossed. Assess those against the three interceptions he has thrown.

Examine his total offense average of 464 yards per game. Note that it would rank him 42nd among 128 Division I bowl subdivision teams, five spots ahead of Clemson, whom Louisville will visit Saturday night.

Notice that Jackson has averaged 131.5 rushing yards per game, more than double the average of Clemson star running back Wayne Gallman.

Observe that Jackson has compiled 25 touchdowns and his team has averaged 682 yards and 63.5 points per game.

Peruse that list, and Jackson's figures would be more believable on a video game – if Louisville discovered a cheat code, accessed his player profile and maxed out his ratings.

Accuracy. Acceleration. Agility. Awareness. Juke. Speed. Power. Speed. They all appear to be locked at 99.

And right now, Jackson is pushing all the right buttons.

Granted, Charlotte and Marshall are not exactly defensive juggernauts. Among Louisville's first four foes, Florida State is the only team ranked in the Top 90 in the bowl subdivision in total defense. Excluding the 663 yards it surrendered to Louisville, Charlotte still would be No. 91.

Yet, on average, Louisville has gained 303 yards above its opponents' total defense average against other foes. Syracuse allowed an average of 340.7 yards against its other three opponents. It allowed 845 to Louisville.

Jackson's rapid rise is startling, considering he appeared in 12 games last season as a freshman but could not seize the starting role.

But there was no cheat code. Evidently, Jackson simply spent the offseason engrossed in his playbook. He coupled his brilliant athleticism with comfort and command of the offense. He has slipped through tackles and carved through coverage with apparent ease.

Jackson's dominance has been aided by a collection of explosive wide receivers. James Quick, Jamari Staples and Jaylen Smith each average more than 22 yards per reception. Running back Brandon Radcliff has averaged 106.8 rushing yards per game.

Louisville looks polished. Louisville looks unstoppable. Louisville looks like what Clemson was expected to be this season.

Clemson has yet to find its groove. Louisville rides an unremitting rhythm.

Louisville quarterback Lamar Jackson shifts to avoid being tackled by Clemson's Ryan Carter during the Tigers' October 1 game against the Cardinals. (Getty Images)

Clemson quarterback Deshaun Watson opened the offseason as the frontrunner for major national awards. Jackson is now the Heisman darling.

Clemson was projected to win the Atlantic Coast Conference. Louisville is now the league's favorite.

Louisville has placed Clemson's defense in a comfortable position. Clemson thrives as the underdog. It thrives when it does not need to fabricate slights.

Despite being ranked in the Top 5 of the bowl subdivision in pass defense, pass efficiency defense, third down defense and points allowed, the Tigers are not expected to contain the Cardinals.

How Clemson responds to that challenge will determine if the Tigers have the substance to withstand the spotlight.

The stage provides the perfect platform for both teams.

Jackson could amplify his Heisman campaign. Watson could rekindle his.

The Tigers could affirm their defensive dominance. Louisville could assert theirs.

Louisville could claim control of the Atlantic Coast Conference. Clemson could protect it.

One of these teams will use this game to propel toward the College Football Playoff. The other will be searching for the reset button. ∎

HEAD COACH
DABO SWINNEY

ESPN GameDay Doesn't Have Anything on Clemson Coach

By Scott Keepfer • October 1, 2016

Last Saturday proved one of the longest days of coach Dabo Swinney's coaching career, but his early morning appearance on ESPN's College GameDay program provided him with a close-up glimpse at the fervor unfolding on the Clemson campus.

It also afforded him the time and opportunity to become Dabo Swinney: Tailgate Crasher.

"When we left GameDay, me and the (state) trooper were going back to Anderson to the hotel," Swinney said. "And coming down Perimeter Road I said, 'Man, pull over here,' and we just stopped at a couple of random tailgates."

Imagine the jaw dropping that occurred when some of the early-arriving fans realized that their impromptu tailgate guest also happened to be the coach of their favorite team.

Rest assured they all enjoyed the moment, even if it did temporarily interrupt one group's beer breakfast.

"This one group had a big orange van, had their chairs kicked back, the doors open and a big-screen TV," Swinney said. "The trooper pulls the car up and they're like, 'What's going on?'

"They're all drinking beer and I roll the window down and say, 'Hey boys, we ready to go?,' and they look at me like, 'Coach Swinney?'"

The stunned group, which included Clemson season ticket holder Eddie Hickman of Inman, his son, Chris, and friend Aaron Roef, had just finished watching Swinney's appearance on ESPN.

"Coach Swinney said, 'What are y'all watching on TV?" Eddie said. "I said, 'Well, about two minutes ago we were watching you.' I was totally shocked. I could hardly speak, and I'm rarely at a loss for words.

"It's just amazing that he took the time on that day to stop and talk to us. It made our day, that's for sure."

Swinney got out of the car and shared handshakes and mugged for photos.

"Y'all are drinking beer already?" Swinney said. "It's gonna be rockin' in the Valley tonight!"

Without hesitation, Hickman replied, "You're absolutely correct, sir!"

Swinney then took his surprise tailgate tour a bit farther up Perimeter Road, where he asked the trooper to pull over again where he saw a couple backed up under a tree, food on the grill, relaxing in their reclining zero-gravity chairs.

"It was the ultimate set-up," Swinney said. "She's got a pillow and covers and everything was right, and I came walking up and I'm like, 'Can I get y'all anything?'"

Swinney joined them for a few minutes, even reclining in one of their chairs.

Dabo Swinney argues with an official during Clemson's win over Louisville. (Bart Boatwright/The Greenville News)

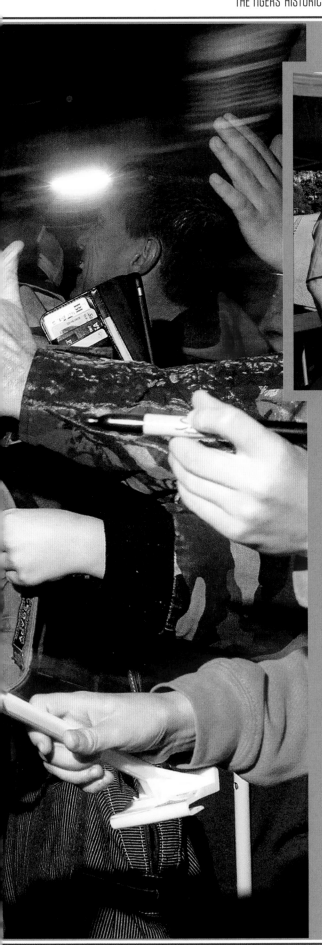

When Swinney rejoined his team back at the hotel, he shared his experience.

"I told them when I got back that it was unbelievable – that there was no telling how early those people were there," Swinney said. "And it's just amazing just to be a part of it. That's what makes Clemson special.

"It's a unique and special place, that's for sure. I don't know how many people were here that weren't even in the stadium; there might have been 15,000-plus just tailgating who didn't come into the stadium."

Swinney said that "Tiger Walk" also provided an indication that it might be a special night on the field as well.

"It was just incredible," said Swinney, whose team knocked off previously unbeaten Louisville 42-36. "You could feel the intensity in the crowd. This was the highest-ranked win we've ever had here. It was a big doggone game and the emotion that was in the crowd – the energy – was powerful. It was a special environment to be a part of." ∎

Opposite: Dabo Swinney greets fans at Memorial Stadium during the early morning hours after Clemson defeated Ohio State in the Fiesta Bowl. (Ken Ruinard/Independent Mail) Above: Swinney poses for a photo with Clemson fans (from left) Eddie Hickman, Chris Hickman, and Aaron Roef on the morning of Clemson's game against Louisville. (Provided photo/Eddie Hickman)

Players douse Dabo Swinney with Gatorade during the closing seconds of Clemson's win over South Carolina. (Bart Boatwright/The Greenville News)

CLEMSON 42, LOUISVILLE 36
October 1, 2016 • Clemson, South Carolina

Clemson Holds On to Knock Off Louisville

Tigers Improve to 5-0

By Scott Keepfer

Clemson quarterback Deshaun Watson threw five touchdown passes, but it was Clemson's defense that saved the game – and perhaps the season – for the Tigers Saturday night.

Cornerback Marcus Edmond knocked Louisville's James Quick out of bounds at the 3-yard line on a fourth-down play with 33 seconds to play as No. 3 Clemson remained unbeaten with a 42-36 Atlantic Coast Conference victory against the No. 4 Cardinals in front of a raucous crowd of 83,362 at Memorial Stadium.

Clemson, which improved to 5-0 overall and 2-0 in the ACC, won its school-record 19th consecutive home game. Louisville (4-1, 2-1 ACC) remained winless in three games against Clemson since joining the ACC three years ago.

All three of the games have been decided by seven points or less, and Saturday night's result was reminiscent of the teams' first meeting in 2014, when Clemson stopped Louisville on a fourth-down play at the 2-yard line to clinch a 23-17 victory.

On Saturday night, Clemson's defense was stifling in the first half, sacking Louisville quarterback Lamar Jackson – who had only been sacked three times in the Cardinals' first four games – four times in the first half.

The Tigers' offense also showed up, building a 28-10 halftime lead on Watson touchdown passes to Deon Cain (twice) and Artavis Scott and a 24-yard scoring run by Wayne Gallman. Watson closed the first half by going 8-for-8 through the air for 152 yards and three scores.

But Jackson and the Cardinals' high-powered offense responded in a big way in the second half, scoring 26 unanswered points to grab a 36-28 lead with 7:52 remaining.

Yet it was Watson and the Clemson offense that had the final say. Artavis Scott's 77-yard kickoff return set up Watson's 20-yard touchdown pass to Mike Williams with 7:06 left, then after Clemson's defense forced a three-and-out, Watson completed 5-of-6 passes on a game-winning 85-yard drive that culminated with a 31-yard strike from Watson to tight end Jordan Leggett.

Watson completed 20 of 31 passes for 306 yards and rushed 14 times for 91 yards while Gallman had 110 yards on 16 carries.

Jackson completed 27 of 44 passes for 295 yards and

Defensive tackle Scott Pagano (right) celebrates with Christian Wilkins after sacking Louisville quarterback Lamar Jackson in the first quarter. (Bart Boatwright/The Greenville News)

a touchdown. He also rushed for 162 yards on 31 carries, including two for touchdowns.

Senior linebacker Ben Boulware was a force, logging a career-high 18 tackles, including three tackles for loss, while safety Van Smith had 16 stops.

Clemson held Louisville to 27 1/2 points below its scoring average and 114 yards below its average yardage. The Cardinals averaged 5.7 yards per play while Clemson averaged 8.2 yards per play.

Greenville's Zykiesis Cannon, a junior safety out of Carolina Academy, had eight tackles for Louisville, including one tackle for loss. ∎

Opposite: Wayne Gallman carries the ball downfield during the third quarter. Clemson's running back rushed for 110 yards on 16 carries. (Bart Boatwright/The Greenville News) Above: Tight end Jordan Leggett made amends for an earlier fumble by catching the go-ahead touchdown in the fourth quarter. (Getty Images)

Resounding Win Points Clemson Toward ACC Title, Playoff

Tigers Poised to Continue Title Run

By Mandrallius Robinson • October 3, 2016

A sense of urgency snapped through the air inside Clemson Memorial Stadium on Saturday night. It fused into a concoction of cautious optimism and anxious apprehension. Clemson fans knew what was at stake.

It was more than fourth and seven. It was more than a conference game. It was more than primetime television.

It was the fleeting opportunity for a return trip to the College Football Playoff. It was the promise of prominence. It was the dream of a national championship.

Louisville quarterback Lamar Jackson was one more dazzling play away from turning the remainder of Clemson's season into a series of exhibition games.

Clemson fans channeled their urgency, their optimism and their apprehension through a defiant roar that no quarterback's cadence could counter.

They understood it was more than fourth-and-seven. They helped turn it into fourth-and-12.

With 40 seconds remaining, the ball resting at the Clemson nine-yard line and the Clemson crowd singing a deafening sonata, Louisville committed its fifth false start of the game. On the ensuing play, after backing up five yards, Jackson completed a pass to James Quick. He sped toward the end zone, but Clemson defensive back Marcus Edmond forced him out of bounds at the three-yard line.

One yard short of the first-down marker.

Death Valley erupted with unbridled relief. Just like Jackson repeatedly slipped the grasp of its defenders, Clemson slipped the clutch of impending disappointment.

A loss would not have ended the season, but Clemson fans appeared to recognize the opportunity at hand.

They recognize the reasonable presumption that junior quarterback Deshaun Watson will proceed to the National Football League after this season. They recognize that he will take many of his offensive weapons to the draft with him. They recognize the heart of the defense, Ben Boulware, will graduate. They recognize the random reach of the coaching carousel that is already spinning.

They recognize that the fortune of the future is curbed by uncertainty. They recognize the promise of the present.

Clemson has fortified the foundation of a perennial contender, like Alabama and Ohio State, who can lose first-round draft picks but not lose a beat. But there is no time like right now.

Clemson enjoyed the taste of glory in the Playoff last year. It fell short in the national championship game, but the work to return started before the team loaded the buses in Arizona.

Clemson has elevated to the echelon of expectation. The stakes are higher. The goal is singular.

It is Playoff or punt.

That is the reward for progress, but it is coupled with immense pressure.

Clemson acknowledged it as they struggled but

With Louisville having scored 26 unanswered points, Artavis Scott's 77-yard kickoff return came at the perfect time for Clemson. (Bart Boatwright/The Greenville News)

survived the first four weeks of this season. This victory is a pivot point.

Clemson seized control of the Atlantic Coast Conference Atlantic Division, while overcoming the toughest challenge remaining on its schedule. Regardless of how far they advance this season, the Tigers will not face a better quarterback. There are not many defenses as tough.

Not in Boston College. Not in Pittsburgh. Not in Wake Forest. And not even in Florida State.

Louisville deserved its Top 5 ranking. And after conquering the Cardinals, Clemson proved that it deserves a Top 4 ranking.

It was not a perfect performance. Clemson has played five games but has not yet played a perfect one. It most likely will not produce one this season.

But Clemson has won each of its five games, and a perfect record is more important than a perfect performance.

Now, the urgency, optimism and apprehension must be channeled into the effort to maintain that unblemished record.

The sluggish start that induced doubt through the previous four weeks will be forgiven. No one will remember the five turnovers the Tigers committed Saturday night. No one will count Watson's interceptions. No one will recall the missed tackles.

Those who witnessed – and perhaps contributed to – Clemson's victory will not forget the thrill of that fourth-down stop. They will not forget the elation of that eruption. They will not forget the roar that will echo to Boston, Winston-Salem, Tallahassee and even Orlando.

They will not forget what is at stake. ∎

#13 WIDE RECEIVER
HUNTER RENFROW

Close Family Helps Receiver Build Confidence

By Brad Senkiw • September 6, 2016

Jordan Renfrow and the rest of his siblings don't care that Hunter Renfrow caught two touchdown passes for Clemson in the national championship game against Alabama.

When they're all together, Hunter doesn't get to call "dibs" just because he's a starting receiver on one of the most talented receiving corps in all of college football.

"That means nothing to us that he's Hunter Renfrow," the second oldest brother of the Renfrow family said. "He can get in line and take his turn.

"That is a neat part of our family. Hunter doesn't see himself as better than anyone. If he tried to pull something over on us at home, it wouldn't work for a second."

And this is one competitive family. Tim Renfrow, the father, was a very successful coach at Socastee High School in Myrtle Beach for 10 years. All four of his sons played at the school, even after Tim moved from the sidelines into the athletic director role. The Renfrows' youngest daughter, Joy, is a "pretty good" high school tennis player, Hunter says.

"I think (older brothers Ayers and Jordan) had a lot of influence on him," Tim said. "We've got a close family.

We've done a lot of things together. The kids were pretty much always together. They fed off each other. They always competed."

Tim never imposed football on his children. He wants his four sons and two daughters to be successful in whatever they do, but around the Renfrow house and their Myrtle Beach neighborhood, sports have meant everything.

"That's how we battled," Hunter said. "My mom (Suzanne) would never let us get in fights, so if we were going to rough up the other one we had to do it in sports. Whether it were the basketball court, you get mad at them, put your shoulder into him and finish. That's just how we did things."

And it's how Hunter began proving himself. He was quite accomplished in high school, earning several awards, including an all-area player of the year honor. But Hunter never had the recruiting stars and hype. He walked on at Clemson, where Jordan, his mother and older sister Chelsea all earned degrees. Hunter redshirted in 2014, but earned a scholarship in the summer of 2015 before he ever caught a pass.

Hunter Renfrow, a walk-on who earned a scholarship before the 2015 season, emerged as a key offensive weapon for the Tigers. (Bart Boatwright/The Greenville News)

Long before Hunter had to make the Clemson team, he first had to show he could handle himself in the backyard, where he learned his competitive drive from his family.

When he was a kid, he wanted to play baseball, another sport he would go on to excel in, with his older brothers and their friends. However, they wouldn't let him join a team until he was able to hit a home run.

"That definitely made me better because I wanted to play with them," Hunter said. "It is a little similar (earning a role at Clemson). You realize you can play with them so you go out there and make the most of your opportunities."

In high school football, Hunter began playing multiple positions on both sides of the ball as a 10th-grader because he was clearly one of the best athletes on the team, not because he was the coach's son, Tim said.

"I remember that I would run what I thought would be a perfect play. We'd execute it well and we'd get eight yards," said Jordan, who as a senior shared the QB role at Socastee with Hunter. "I thought that was pretty good. Then Hunter would come in, run the wrong play, run the opposite direction he was supposed to and break it for 80 (yards). That was typical Hunter Renfrow."

Nobody thought Renfrow's days at Socastee would turn him into a slot receiver for a national title contender. At 5-foot-11, 180 pounds, Hunter is the smallest brother in the house. He was the quietest growing up, yet he's the one playing big-time football.

Tim believes Hunter's lack of stature is a reason for where he is today.

"That's something you don't talk about a lot, but it's an inner thing that really drives him," Tim said. "He wants to show people that size really doesn't matter that much if you've got the desire and passion and work ethic."

Jordan, who knows as well as anybody the kind of athlete his younger brother is, didn't have a good feeling about Hunter's chances at making Dabo Swinney's squad. He was a student at Clemson when NFL receivers Sammy Watkins and Martavis Bryant were running wild.

"Hunter's a good player, but he's never going to play at Clemson. I point blank said that, that he's not that good," Jordan said when recalling a conversation he had with a friend. "Even when talk started of him going to Clemson, I didn't think he would be a football star at all – by any means."

The Renfrow parents were also caught off guard in Week 3 last season. Tim says the Clemson coaches told them right before last year's Louisville game that Hunter would be in the rotation, so Tim and Suzanne, who also works at Socastee High, took off to Kentucky on a Wednesday. They're glad they did, as Hunter caught his first career touchdown that Thursday night. However, they had to get back to Myrtle Beach in time to watch Cole, their youngest son, play a high school game that Friday.

After that, there were many more trips to book.

"It was a lot of traveling, but it was fun," Tim said.

The Renfrows have been going to football games together for more than a decade, but now they're enjoying new bonding experiences through Clemson and Hunter's successes.

They turned the national title game into a huge family vacation in January. They were in the stands, minus Chelsea, at the season opener at Auburn on Saturday, when Hunter made a leaping, 16-yard touchdown grab in the end zone on Clemson's final scoring drive of a close, 19-13 win.

"It was fun. It was exciting, I'm glad it turned out that way," Suzanne said of being there for the spectacular catch.

If Hunter keeps scoring touchdowns for one of the top-ranked teams in the country, the Renfrows will be spending even more time together, supporting their budding collegiate star, who remains grounded in family.

"My girlfriend still treats me the same. My family still treats me the same. Not much has changed," Hunter said. "I'm still the same person." ■

Hunter Renfrow gets a hug from his girlfriend, Camilla Martin, after Clemson's season-opening win over Auburn. (Ken Ruinard/Independent Mail)

CLEMSON 56, BOSTON COLLEGE 10

October 7, 2016 • Chestnut Hill, Massachusetts

Offense Heats Up

Clemson Shows No Sign of Letdown, Rolls Boston College

By Brad Senkiw

Clemson's offense is getting cranked up.

There was a time, namely before Friday night's game at Boston College, when the Tigers were last in the ACC in plays of 40 yards or more.

In fact, they had only produced one play in that range and none of 50 yards or more.

Those numbers lasted for about 13 and a half minutes at Alumni Stadium.

The No. 3 Tigers produced three plays of at least 50 yards or more and scored three touchdowns all in the first quarter in an easy, 56-10 win over the Eagles.

"We just hit some big plays and got control of the game pretty early," Clemson head coach Dabo Swinney said. "The execution was tremendous, outside of a couple of snafus like at the end of the first half. Dominant second half and that was good to see."

Clemson showed no effects of an emotional letdown coming off last week's big win over Louisville or the difficulty of preparing during a short week.

Clemson (6-0, 3-0 ACC) improved to 8-1 against BC under Swinney behind a balanced offense that picked up right where it left off last week when it produced 507 yards against Louisville.

"Just really proud of them. It's our eighth consecutive road win, which ties a Clemson record. I've been doing this a long time," Swinney said. "There's a reason that record is only eight. It's really hard to do. Just proud of our team for coming up here and getting themselves ready."

Against Boston College's top-ranked total defense, Clemson racked up 261 total yards in the first half, when it built a 21-3 lead despite a scoreless second quarter. The Tigers finished with 499 total yards.

Wayne Gallman, who had 109 yards on nine carries, got it started when he ripped off a 59-yard touchdown run on Clemson's second drive of the game for a 7-0 lead.

On its next possession, Deshaun Watson found Mike Williams on a 50-yard pass that Williams laid out to haul in. That set up a 9-yard strike from Watson to Williams that put Clemson up 14-3 with 3:12 left in the first quarter.

The Tigers weren't done. Tight end Jordan Leggett caught a short Watson pass, made a couple cuts and went 56 yards for the touchdown on the only play of the drive with 1:29 left in the first quarter.

"The three plays of 50-plus yards in the first quarter against the No. 1 defense in the country was just tremendous execution and some just want to," Swinney said. "The balance of our offense was tremendous, run for 200-plus, pass for 200-plus, set up all of our play-actions. Our ability to run the football was critical."

The Eagles (3-3, 0-3) came into the game having

Mike Williams extends past Boston College cornerback Isaac Yiadom to catch a 50-yard pass in the first quarter. (Bart Boatwright/The Greenville News)

given up just two plays from 50 yards or more all year, and they were only allowing 124 passing yards per game.

Watson had that in the first 15 minutes, and he finished with 266 yards on 14-of-24 passing and four touchdowns for an offense that's looking more like the one from last year than the one that started slow in 2016.

"Once we connect on those passes and do the little things right, the big things open up," said Watson, who added 28 rushing yards. "Once we start clicking, it's hard to stop us."

Clemson receiver Deon Cain was on the receiving end of a pair of third quarter TD strikes from 29 and 16 yards.

The Clemson offense did post another big play late in the game when freshman running back Tavien Feaster went 49 yards for a TD run.

It was the second consecutive year that BC came into this divisional showdown with a top-ranked defense, but ended up struggling against Watson and the Tigers.

This year, the Eagles had not faced an offense like this against Georgia Tech, UMass, Wagner and Buffalo. Virginia Tech did throw for 256 yards against BC, though.

Clemson made it look easy for the most part. The Tigers did struggle some in the second quarter when they went 0-for-3 on third-down conversions, and by the fourth quarter, when they led 42-10, the stars were done for the night.

The Clemson defense got a fourth-quarter, 42-yard pick-six from Mark Fields, and it held BC out of the end zone until the third quarter when Bobby Wolford caught a 1-yard TD pass from Patrick Towles.

The Tigers overcame an early hole when Ray-Ray McCloud fumbled a punt return deep in BC territory, but Clemson's defense held the Eagles to a field goal, despite them having first-and-goal.

BC, which finished with 251 total yards, was outmatched for much of the night on both sides of the ball, and the Eagles extended their 11-game ACC losing streak with the loss.

"I thought we played pretty spirited in the first half," BC head coach Steve Addazio said. "Really felt like we should have been (down) 21-10 at halftime. We let up some big plays, a few big plays, but aside from a couple of big plays, we were playing hard, playing fast and right in the middle of that game." ∎

Jordan Leggett races downfield to score a touchdown in the first quarter. Clemson's tight end went 56 yards on the play. (Bart Boatwright/The Greenville News)

#99 DEFENSIVE END
CLELIN FERRELL

Defensive End Battles Back from Injuries, Tragic Events

By Dan Hope • October 11, 2016

Clelin Ferrell's road to starting at defensive end for the Clemson football team hasn't come easily. When Ferrell was 14, his father died after a battle with cancer.

Before his senior season of high school, Ferrell suffered a knee injury that kept him out of action for two full years.

In life and on the football field, Ferrell has had to deal with uncertainty, but that hasn't stopped him from becoming a key player on Clemson's defensive line as a redshirt freshman. He has started every game for the Tigers this season, has become one of the team's top pass-rushers and might just be scratching the surface of his potential.

His Toughest Loss

Ferrell said the death of his father was the hardest thing he has had to deal with.

Fortunately, he had many role models to help him through. These included his mother, seven older siblings and his instructors, including football coach Greg Lilly, at Benedictine College Prep, the all-boys' Catholic military high school he attended in Richmond, Virginia.

It wasn't easy to lose the man he described as the rock of the family.

"I didn't get a chance to go through my teenage years with him," Ferrell said. "He was a really, really good person in my life, and everybody liked that he was in it."

As Ferrell adapted to life without his father while his mother adapted to life without her husband, they would get into more arguments than normal.

"I became a little bit rebellious just because I was confused on the situation," Ferrell said. "It's hard dealing with somebody who was so steady in your life, and now they're just completely gone."

Faye Ferrell said while her son acted out at times, he learned from his mistakes.

"He was no angel," Faye said. "But if he did ever go astray, it wasn't hard to bring him back."

One thing Ferrell and his father bonded over during their years together was a mutual love of sports, especially football.

As Ferrell coped with his loss, he emerged as a star on the football field.

Clelin Ferrell (left) celebrates with defensive back Ryan Carter (center) after Clemson sacked Georgia Tech quarterback Justin Thomas during the fourth quarter of Clemson's September 22 win. (Bart Boatwright/The Greenville News)

Upside Recognized

It was during a middle school jamboree that Byron Ferrell, Clelin's second-oldest brother, recognized his brother had the potential to be a great football player.

"He was getting double-teamed, and he was kind of complaining," Byron said. "I said, 'Look man … they're double-teaming you because you're good. It's a compliment. You just get out there and rip it up out there.' And he went back out there and he just blew the whole offense up. Just blasting through every time, sacks, played like a mad man out there. He was like a high school player playing with little kids."

It was at the start of Ferrell's sophomore year, just months after his father died, that Lilly recognized Ferrell had the talent to be special.

"The first game he played in for us on the varsity his sophomore year, he had three sacks, five tackles for a loss and we said, 'Yeah, he's a little different than everybody else,'" Lilly said.

By the end of his junior year, Ferrell had emerged as one of the top high school defensive ends in the nation, and was recruited by top colleges.

Ferrell grew up as a huge Virginia Tech fan, which was among the schools that offered him, but he ultimately chose Clemson before his senior year.

He decided to become a Tiger because of the strong bonds he built with Clemson's coaching staff, including defensive coordinator Brent Venables.

"When I got to Clemson, it was just a different feeling," Ferrell said. "When I saw Clemson, I was like 'Wow, this is the place for me,' because the people here definitely are like a family."

Return from Injury

An all-state selection for Benedictine in his junior year, when he recorded 26 tackles for a loss, Ferrell showed flashes of being even better in his senior year.

"He played in a scrimmage and a half (before the season), and people couldn't even get their hands on him," Lilly said. "The first scrimmage, we took him out of it after probably two or three series, because it just wasn't fair."

During the second quarter of Benedictine's second scrimmage, Ferrell's season ended before it ever began. He was trying to chase down a scrambling quarterback when he tore his ACL.

"When I planted to make an angle, my knee just went in and just gave out, popped, and this instant feeling of just fire in my leg … I had never been hurt before, so it was just like, I don't know what's going on right now," Ferrell said.

Sitting on the sidelines and watching his team win a state championship was tough.

It took him more than a year to fully recover from the injury, so he ended up redshirting his first year at Clemson. Watching the Tigers play for a national championship wasn't any easier.

"It was a tough process," Ferrell said. "There were ups and there were downs and there was some times where I was confused. You have those doubts of 'Well, what if I get injured again?' or just when I was in camp last year, just some times I didn't feel like I was able to compete at the highest level with these guys."

Now that the injury is behind him, Ferrell is proving he can compete at the highest level.

Rising Star

Clemson coach Dabo Swinney says he is really pleased with the way Ferrell has performed this season.

"He's a really quiet guy off the field … but he plays loud," Swinney said. "He's got a very bright future here. Incredibly bright. Because he's just going to get better in my opinion."

Since arriving at Clemson, Ferrell has worked to get

Clelin Ferrell emerged as one of Clemson's top pass rushers in 2016. (Bart Boatwright/The Greenville News)

to where he can contribute on a regular basis.

"He's really worked for everything that he's gotten," Venables said. "He's very, very coachable, and never satisfied."

Clemson's coaches agree that Ferrell has a high ceiling. Defensive ends coach Marion Hobby said before the season that he would compare Ferrell to former Ohio State defensive end Will Smith, who went on to be a first-round NFL draft pick by the New Orleans Saints,

where Hobby coached him for two years.

Ferrell has had to overcome obstacles to get to where he is, but he believes that has made him a stronger person. And he is more appreciative of his ability to play the game than he had ever been before.

"This is the most fun I've ever had playing football in my life, and I feel like people can see that," Ferrell said. "I didn't understand how much I loved football until it was taken away." ■

CLEMSON 24, N.C. STATE 17 (OT)
October 15, 2016 • Clemson, South Carolina

Edmond, and Clemson, Can Breathe Again

Tigers Outlast Wolfpack in Overtime Thriller

By Scott Keepfer

The Clemson postgame tradition of "Gathering at the Paw" gave way to a dogpile in the end zone Saturday afternoon.

At the bottom of it was Marcus Edmond.

"I almost died," Edmond said.

So, too, did Clemson's national championship hopes.

Clemson prevailed against N.C. State Saturday afternoon at Memorial Stadium by slipping past the Wolfpack by the slimmest of margins, winning a taught, tense, 24-17 thriller when a 33-yard field goal attempt by State's Kyle Bambard sailed a couple of feet wide on the final play of regulation, giving the Tigers new life.

Clemson capitalized, as quarterback Deshaun Watson, as he is wont to do, flashed his composure by firing a bullet to a sliding Artavis Scott for the winning touchdown in overtime.

Seconds later, the Wolfpack's first play of overtime became its last. Edmond leaped and came down with Ryan Finley's pass attempt to Bra'Lon Cherry in the end zone, the ball – and Clemson's immediate future – clutched firmly in his hands.

"Everybody kept piling on me, and I couldn't breathe," Edmond said after logging his first career interception at the most opportune of times.

And because of Edmond, 82,104 fans packed into Death Valley suddenly could.

"Just another day at the office," Clemson coach Dabo Swinney said. "We wanted to be sure ABC's coast-to-coast ratings went up."

For much of the game, Clemson's ratings struggled to hold steady. N.C. State forced four Clemson turnovers, giving the Tigers nine in their last two home games, and working the Tigers' defense for several long drives, primarily behind the running of Matthew Dayes, who was as advertised and finished with 106 yards.

But much like what transpired in the Louisville game two weeks ago, Clemson's defense shined brightest at the end.

"Marcus Edmond executed on the last plays of the game for two consecutive (home) games and made two of the biggest plays we're probably ever going to have," Swinney said.

Instead of having to explain away a loss to an unranked N.C. State team, Clemson wound up extending its home winning streak to a school-record 20 consecutive games – the longest active streak in

Defensive back K'Von Wallace (right) celebrates with defensive lineman Clelin Ferrell after Wallace's interception in the second quarter. (Bart Boatwright/The Greenville News)

the nation. The Tigers also have won 13 ACC games in a row, which matches the nation's longest active conference winning streak.

"At the end of the day, we're 7-0 and the only team in the Atlantic Division that controls their destiny, and that's where we wanted to be," Swinney said.

Clemson, whose last loss to an unranked opponent came against N.C. State in 2011, got another big game from Watson, who completed a school-record 39 passes in 52 attempts for 378 yards.

Mike Williams was his favored target, contributing 146 yards on a career-best 12 receptions.

The Tigers' latest victory wrote yet another chapter in the Book of Watson, and illustrated once again how the difference between unbeaten and heartbroken can be miniscule.

Just ask Dabo Swinney.

And Dave Doeren.

"First of all, I have to give N.C. State a lot of credit," Swinney said. "We knew they were going to give us every ounce of juice that they had in their body, and they did.

"We've had nine turnovers in our last two home games here, but obviously we're finding ways to win against good teams."

Doeren took no solace in the close defeat.

"Two years ago it was 41-0," said Doeren, N.C. State's fourth-year head coach. "Today we played them into overtime with a chance to beat them and we didn't. It was not a moral victory…we could have won that game. We were one play away from having a masterpiece today, and we just didn't."

It wasn't a masterpiece for Clemson, either, but when N.C. State's final-second field goal slid right, the picture the Tigers' painted Saturday suddenly looked a lot more appealing.

"I couldn't even watch," senior tight end Jordan Leggett said. "I had my face in my towel praying, and somebody up above was looking out for us."

No argument there. ■

Defensive back Marcus Edmond intercepts a pass intended for Wolfpack receiver Bra'Lon Cherry in overtime to secure the Tigers' 24-17 win. (Bart Boatwright/The Greenville News)

CLEMSON 37, FLORIDA STATE 34
October 29, 2016 • Tallahassee, Florida

Watson and Tigers End Up On Top, Again

QB Continues Trend of Late-Game Heroics Against FSU

By Scott Keepfer

Deshaun Watson began building his reputation as a big-time college quarterback two years ago in an overtime loss at Florida State.

He cemented it Saturday night – again at Florida State, but this time in a victory.

Watson shrugged off two interceptions and proved his mettle once more in crunch time, guiding Clemson on three scoring drives in the fourth quarter in a 37-34 victory at Doak Campbell Stadium.

In his second and final game in the stadium, Watson staged a farewell worthy of the scrapbook, accounting for 430 yards.

He completed 27 of 43 passes, matching his season-high with 378 yards. He also rushed a season-high 17 times for 52 yards and became the first Clemson quarterback – and just the fourth overall – to defeat Florida State in back to back years.

"That's special," Watson said. "Coach (Dabo) Swinney told me about that Friday night. (N.C. State's) Philip Rivers did it, and I can't remember the other two guys, but it's special to be in that group. It's hard to win, especially against these guys, and especially back to back."

Watson got off to an auspicious start Saturday night, guiding the Tigers to touchdown drives on their first two possessions for a 14-0 lead. But things got a bit testy after that.

On Clemson's fourth drive of the game, early in the third quarter, Watson was intercepted by the Seminoles' Marquez White – Watson's first career interception against the Seminoles. It proved costly, as Florida State drove 60 yards in six plays for a touchdown.

In the third quarter, Watson was intercepted again at the Tigers' 43-yard line. Florida State's Dalvin Cook dashed 43 yards for a score on the next play as the Seminoles took their first lead of the game, 21-20. Following another Cook run, this time for 70 yards out, Florida State led 28-20 entering the final quarter.

"I made two boneheaded decisions," Watson said. "I just tried to get greedy."

Watson made amends.

He completed 8 of 13 passes for 137 yards and a touchdown in the final period, solidifying his reputation as a late-game miracle worker. Saturday night marked his third fourth-quarter comeback this season. Over his career, Watson is 104 for 155 for 1,280 yards and 13 touchdown with just one interception; that translates to

Safety Jadar Johnson flies in front of Seminoles receiver Auden Tate to intercept a pass in the second quarter. (Ken Ruinard/Independent Mail)

a completion percentage of 67.0 and a passing efficiency rating of 162.9.

"He's got the heart of a champion," co-offensive coordinator Tony Elliott said. "The thing I love about Deshaun, he doesn't crumble, he doesn't break when he has a mistake.

"He just keeps on playing, keeps on swinging, and that's what why you see good things happen for him. I feel blessed to have the best quarterback in the country."

As this season has progressed so, too, has Watson. Saturday's night's performance was his fourth 300-yard passing game in the last five, and he has now thrown at least one touchdown pass in 25 consecutive games – a school record and the longest active streak in the nation.

"He's just unbelievable," Swinney said. "He just keeps playing. And that fourth quarter was just awesome."

Watson, who's now 26-2 as a starter in his career, appeared to take it all in stride.

"There's going to be adversity, but the game wasn't over," Watson said. "And at the end of the day it's about being on top at the end of the game." ◼

Opposite: Deshaun Watson became the first Clemson quarterback to defeat Florida State in back to back years. (Bart Boatwright/The Greenville News) Above: Wide receiver Trevion Thompson holds on to a reception in the second quarter. (Ken Ruinard/Independent Mail)

This Is Who You Are, Clemson. Embrace the Anxiety.

Fans Getting Used to Last-Minute Heroics

By Mandrallius Robinson • October 31, 2016

ill your heroes escape the clutches of the evil villain? Can they elude another near defeat from the depths of despair?

Tune in next week, Clemson University fans.

This program is brought to you by Dabo Swinney blood pressure monitors, when your heart can barely stand the excitement. By Greg Huegel blindfolds, when you cannot bear to watch the kick. And by Brent Venables' All-Out Blitz energy drinks, when you need a boost on fourth down.

Clemson has produced a thrilling dramatic series through eight games, and its most important rating is still perfect. Instead of longing for a script with fewer plot twists and less daring stunts, it may be time for Clemson fans to accept and embrace this show.

This week's episode featured the desperado Dalvin Cook as he tied Victory to the railroad tracks near the Tallahassee station. In the final scene, the gallant protagonists arrived in their white uniforms and whisked Victory away just before the Seminole Express rumbled by.

Most defensive coordinators would have opted to play it safe, rush three and drop eight cautiously in coverage. For Venables, caution was too risky.

With Florida State needing a Hail Mary ... a rabbit's foot, a four-leaf clover and a presidential pardon ... on fourth-and-22 at its own 44-yard line, Venables blitzed both inside linebackers. Ben Boulware corralled quarterback Deondre Francois for an 11-yard sack.

Clemson's aggressive call helped the Tigers outlast another brush with disaster. The heroes rode away with

Victory into the Tallahassee twilight.

But these heroes are conflicted characters.

The trailers that aired constantly during the summer highlighted Heisman Trophy finalist quarterback Deshaun Watson and his gang of All-Americans. They were expected to carve smoothly through the schedule, mask the inexperienced defense and close the season with another showdown with Alabama.

However, the offense has struggled with bouts of inefficiency and sporadic spells of turnovers. The defense has been a forceful unit but has endured its own set of blunders.

With edgy swagger and steely resolve, Clemson has advanced in spite of its miscues. Saturday night, the Tigers faltered on both sides of the ball, but, at the crest of crisis, they thrived.

Untimely lapses and a relegation of the running game negated the offense's furious opening. Watson tossed a pair of interceptions, but in the fourth quarter, he completed seven of 11 attempts for 127 yards and led a pair of scoring drives.

The defense's aggressive coverage provoked five pass interference penalties. Some were questionable. Others were inexcusable. Clemson allowed Cook to rush for 120 yards and two touchdowns in the third quarter alone, but in the fourth, Cook mustered merely 16.

It may never be pretty. It may never be easy. It may never be predictable.

But no one can say it is not entertaining.

We have been waiting for the Tigers to snap out of their funk. We have been waiting for them to dominate

Cheering for Clemson was not for the faint of heart during the first two months of the 2016 season. (Ken Ruinard/ Independent Mail)

perceived inferior foes. We have been waiting for them to establish their rhythm and waltz back to the College Football Playoff.

At this point, we must realize that the dazzling dance that carried Clemson to prominence last year did not carry over to this season. It simply set a standard by which Clemson is assessed, beyond wins and losses and perhaps beyond reason.

We are still waiting for something to click. We are still waiting on some grand awakening. We are still waiting on Clemson to become the marvels of their preseason promotions.

Clemson fans should wait no longer on that lofty ideal. For the sake of your own mental wellbeing, embrace these complex characters, even if you have to watch nervously through your fingers.

The run to perfection has not been perfect, but Clemson has exhibited tenacity, poise and resilience that its opponents have not shown.

If North Carolina State had more of it, the Wolfpack may not have needed to settle for that errant field goal. If Florida State had more of it, the Seminoles may not have committed consecutive false start penalties on their final drive.

If this season is not canceled before the finale in Tampa, Clemson may meet again with the most notorious villain of them all. The Tigers would not be expected to survive a sloppy showing against Alabama, but they already have exposed the folly of declarative expectations.

It may not be optimal. For Clemson and its fans, it certainly is not desirable, but, in each of the remaining episodes, Clemson could wager its fate on the aggressive attitude that has created and eliminated danger.

The lofty ideal may never be reached. The Tigers are not in a funk. They are not in a fog. The heroes are not wearing masks.

This is their identity. This is their rhythm. This is their version of perfection.

Stay tuned. ■

CLEMSON 54, SYRACUSE 0
November 5, 2016 • Clemson, South Carolina

Tigers Put it in Cruise Control Against Syracuse

Watson Sits Out Second Half with Bruised Shoulder

By Scott Keepfer

lose games?

Nail-biting drama?

Who needs it?

Certainly not Clemson, and certainly not Saturday afternoon.

After winning by a touchdown or less in five of its first eight games this season, the Tigers opted for a more relaxing route to victory Saturday at Memorial Stadium.

Clemson bolted to a 30-0 halftime lead and coasted to a 54-0 victory against Syracuse that positioned the Tigers squarely on the doorstep of a second consecutive Atlantic Coast Conference Atlantic Division title.

"It was nice – these last few games we've been holding onto our hats in the fourth quarter," Clemson coach Dabo Swinney said. "It was nice to have a game where we could have some fun and get a bunch of guys into the game."

Um, 85 guys, to be exact, including senior back-up quarterback Nick Schuessler, who performed admirably in relief as Deshaun Watson packed his bruised shoulder on ice after leaving the game for good late in the second quarter.

He'll be fine, Swinney reassured, and his absence Saturday was of little consequence as the Tigers proceeded to put the offense on cruise control and amass a season-high 565 yards of offense.

The defense fairly shined as well, recording its second shutout of the season and fifth since Brent Venables was given the reins to Clemson's defense in 2012.

But the bottom line proved even sweeter – Clemson is 9-0 for a second consecutive season and has two of its final three games at home, where it has won a school-record 21 straight games.

"As we get into November here, we're headed in the right direction," Swinney said. "We talked all week about how we've been at our best in the fourth quarter, and now we're getting into the fourth quarter of the season. Today we started fast and didn't let up all day."

Truer words were never spoken. The Tigers led 10-0 after the first quarter, then used the second quarter to amass 330 yards and 20 more points, allowing the crowd of 80,609 to sit back, take a breath and enjoy the halftime Military Appreciation Day festivities day without fear of an aerial attack by the visitors.

Syracuse quarterback Eric Dungey wasn't as fortunate as Watson. Dungey left the game for good with

Tanner Muse celebrates his 64-yard interception return for a touchdown against Syracuse. (Bart Boatwright/The Greenville News)

3:11 left in the first quarter after absorbing a hard hit at the end of a six-yard run, rendering the Orange offense inconsistent at best, hapless at worst.

Clemson's defense intercepted three Syracuse passes, with the final one returned 64 yards for a touchdown by freshman safety Tanner Muse, and held the Orange to 277 total yards – their lowest output of the season.

"Today they flexed their muscles," Clemson coach Dabo Swinney said. "Our guys were locked in. It was a very crisp day."

It was crisp for the offense, too, which was diverse and efficient. Schuessler completed 11 of 17 passes for a career-high 177 yards and two touchdowns, and the Tigers had two receivers with more than 100 yards receiving – Deon Cain, with five receptions for career-best 125 yards, and Mike Williams, with six catches for 106 yards.

Cain scored two touchdowns, including a 65-yarder from Watson on Clemson's second play of the second quarter that ranks as the Tigers' longest offensive play of the season.

Williams added a 14-yard touchdown catch, Artavis Scott a five-yard scoring reception and Watson and Wayne Gallman added touchdown runs of one and five yards, respectively, for Clemson.

"Obviously we played a fantastic football team in Clemson," Syracuse coach Dino Babers said. "My hat goes off to coach Dabo Swinney. Unbelievable team – offensively, defensively, kicking game. Definitely a team worthy of its ranking and I wish them the best of luck on their goal to win a national championship."

Watson, meanwhile, is expected to play next week when the Tigers host Pittsburgh with a chance to clinch the league's Atlantic Division title at home.

"In control of our destiny is where we wanted to be," Swinney said.

For a sixth straight week, that's precisely where the Tigers find themselves. ◼

Running back C.J. Fuller tries to get past Syracuse defensive back Christopher Fredrick during the first quarter. Clemson led 30-0 at halftime. (Ken Ruinard/Independent Mail)

PITTSBURGH 43, CLEMSON 42
November 12, 2016 • Clemson, South Carolina

Pitt Shocks No. 2 Clemson

Late Field Goal Hands Tigers First Defeat

By Brad Senkiw

Jadar Johnson saved Clemson in Week 1 at Auburn, knocking down two potential touchdown passes in the final seconds.

An on-side kick recovery by the Tigers in Week 2 kept things from getting dicey against Troy.

Marcus Edmond saved the day against Louisville.

Luck, and a raucous crowd, kept N.C. State from drilling a game-winning field goal a month ago.

Jordan Leggett's acrobatic reach and score bested Florida State.

Taunting defeat in five of their first nine games finally caught up to the No. 2 Tigers on Saturday.

Unranked Pittsburgh got a 48-yard field goal from Chris Blewitt with six seconds left to shock Clemson 43-42 at Memorial Stadium, and the dream of perfection ended.

"At the end of the day, it's all about finishing," Clemson coach Dabo Swinney said. "It's my job to put us in a position to finish, and I didn't do that. Where it starts and stops is with me."

Swinney and the Tigers (9-1, 6-1 ACC) vow that the season isn't over. Expectations and goals are still on the table, but it didn't seem that way to a hushed crowd after a four-hour shootout Saturday.

"We're obviously disappointed," Clemson wide receiver Hunter Renfrow said. "We're trying to think about the… positives and moving onto the next game. In life you can't look at the bad stuff and let this game beat us twice next week. We've got to get up and move forward."

The Tigers have to wait until next week's game at Wake Forest to try to clinch the Atlantic Division title for a chance to play in the conference championship Dec. 3 in Orlando.

Swinney, whose team racked up 630 yards but came up empty twice in the red zone, said adversity doesn't build character, it reveals it.

The Tigers will put that to the test as they can still win the division, state title, conference and "closer."

"Every single goal is right there in front of us. Every. Single. Goal," Swinney said.

But what about the College Football Playoff? Michigan and Washington, ranked third and fourth, respectively, in the playoff rankings, also lost Saturday. So Tuesday's newest rankings will be telling.

Will Clemson still be in play in December for a berth?

What isn't alive anymore is Clemson's 45-game winning streak over unranked teams. Saturday was the Tigers' first regular-season loss since a Nov. 15, 2014, loss at Georgia Tech. And a 15-game ACC streak is over too.

"Turnovers caught up with us tonight," Swinney said. "We've had a lot of turnovers, especially in the red zone."

Clemson didn't think it would be in a position to

Deshaun Watson leaves the field after Clemson's disappointing and surprising 43-42 loss to Pitt. Watson threw for 580 yards, three touchdowns and three interceptions in the game. (Ken Ruinard/Independent Mail)

lose to the Panthers (6-4, 3-3). Neither did Vegas, which had the Tigers favored by 22 points at game time.

Too many penalties, a defense that gave up a season high in points and a run game that couldn't close the deal dealt Clemson a fatal blow.

"We've been on the right side all year," Clemson defensive coordinator Brent Venables said. "This one hurts. We were just on the wrong side of it all night. I know what our guys are made of. Our guys will come out swinging and have the kind of focus that we need to."

Deshaun Watson passed for an ACC single-game record 580 yards and tossed three touchdowns on 52 completions. Mike Williams caught 15 passes for 202 yards, both career highs. Wayne Gallman rushed for three touchdowns, but the Tigers managed just 50 yards on the ground, their first game under 100 yards since the Russell Athletic Bowl in 2014.

"You just got to take your hat off to Pitt, their team, their coaches," said Swinney, who lost at home for the first time since 2013. "They hung in there and they made the plays when they needed to make them.

"This one is on me."

Watson threw three interceptions to match his pick total (13) from 2015, and it was his last one that proved the most costly.

Pitt picked off a pass at the Panther goal line and returned it to the Clemson 30, and James Conner, who had 132 rushing yards, scored on a 20-yard TD run with 5:17 to play. The two-point conversion failed, and Clemson took over up 42-40 with 5:17 left in the game.

The Tigers tried to run out the clock but couldn't get one more yard in two tries at the Pitt 35. Swinney didn't hesitate to go for it, but Gallman came up short on fourth down, and the Panthers took over with 58 seconds remaining.

Pitt QB Nate Peterman, who had 308 passing yards and five touchdowns, then rushed for a nine-yard gain before finding Scott Orndoff for 21 of his 128 yards. The Panthers got to the CU 29 with 12 seconds left, and Blewitt split the uprights to shock the Tiger faithful.

"He's been a money kicker," Pitt coach Pat Narduzzi said. "I knelt down with the guys, said a prayer and I had no doubt it was going to go through. It was destiny."

That's something Clemson controls a little less of now. ■

Tight end Jordan Leggett dives near Pitt defensive back Jordan Whitehead after a catch. Leggett had a big game with six catches for 95 yards. (Ken Ruinard/Independent Mail)

CLEMSON 35, WAKE FOREST 13
November 19, 2016• Winston-Salem, North Carolina

Tigers Survive Another Muffed Punt

Clemson Clinches ACC Atlantic Division Title with Win

By Brad Senkiw

For anyone wondering if momentum is a real thing, you don't have to look any farther than No. 5 Clemson's 35-13 win at Wake Forest on Saturday.

The Tigers (10-1, 7-1) clinched the ACC Atlantic Division title on the road, but they made it more interesting than it appeared it would be early in the game.

A muffed punt by Ray-Ray McCloud early in the second quarter stopped a streak of four consecutive Tiger touchdown drives and gave the Demon Deacons (6-5, 3-4) life when they previously had very little.

Clemson coach Dabo Swinney still has faith in McCloud, even though he removed him from punt returns in the second half.

"The first thing we've got to do is put a guy back there who is going to possess the ball, No. 1. He's not playing with a lot of confidence, for whatever reason, back there, and we've got to get him back confident," Swinney said. "He's still a young player who's maturing. I'll tell you this right now – you can write this down – I don't know when Ray-Ray's gonna finish up, but before that guy's out of here he's gonna be as good a punt returner as we've had here. I believe that. But obviously we've got some work to do in instilling the mentality he's

got to have back there."

It led to a field goal by Wake that put it on the board. The next six Clemson drives went like this: turnover on downs, punt, end of half, turnover on downs, punt and punt.

That run ended with a 1-yard touchdown run by Wayne Gallman to put Clemson up 35-13 with 10:50 left in the game.

Before that, though, a Wake offense that had just 27 yards in the first quarter seized momentum to get within two possessions in the second quarter.

Clemson started out hot. Gallman reeled off a 42-yard TD run on fourth-and-inches to put Clemson up 7-0 on the first possession.

Clemson QB Deshaun Watson scored on a 3-yard run to make it a two-touchdown lead before finding Mike Williams on a 15-yard TD pass for a 21-0 advantage before the first quarter even ended.

A few minutes later, Watson trotted into the end zone for his second rushing score, and Clemson was up four touchdowns.

Wake was reeling and looking like a blowout was coming sooner rather than later.

"There definitely was a momentum swing," Clemson

Deshaun Watson scores one of his three touchdowns on the day, one of which came through the air and two on the ground. Clemson dominated Wake Forest in a 35-13 win. (Bart Boatwright/The Greenville News)

co-offensive coordinator Jeff Scott said. "We got off to a really fast start. Wish we would not have given them so much momentum. But proud of the way the guys came out in the second half and finished the game the right way."

McCloud changed that when he was unable to field a high punt with 10:41 left before halftime. It was the second time he was unable to come up with a punt in the first half, and it was Clemson's only turnover of the night. This time, the ball went right through his hands and was recovered by Chuck Wade at the CU 27.

It marked the sixth time this season McCloud has put the ball on the ground on a punt return via a muff or fumble. He received a hard learning lesson against Troy in Week 2 when he dropped the ball while going into the end zone on a big return, and the Trojans recovered it.

He also muffed a punt deep in Boston College territory last month that led to a field goal.

"We'll talk about that when we get back, but it's unfortunate because he is such a talented player," Swinney said. "He's got a job to do and everybody's counting on him to get his job done. It was a critical error right there."

After Wake's first field goal, it forced an incomplete pass on fourth-and-6 to take over at its own 36. Six plays later, Cade Carney plunged into the end zone from a yard out to make it a 28-10 game.

Once Clemson forced a Wake punt in the third quarter, Artavis Scott, not McCloud, was back to return it.

"That was obviously disappointing us giving them the ball down there," Jeff Scott said. "It's a play he's got to be able to make. Unfortunately he wasn't able to get it done and he put it on the ground so we went to Artavis to finish up the game."

The Tigers, who have turned the ball over 22 times this season, never gave up the lead in that game or against Wake. The defense was able to hold the Deacs to three more points the rest of the game and 197 total yards in the win.

"We don't focus on (the momentum shift)," Clemson linebacker Ben Boulware said. "Our players don't look at the situation like, 'They might get some momentum here. They're going to come back and beat us.' We're focusing on every snap." ∎

Defensive lineman Christian Wilkins reacts after a tackle for a loss in the second quarter of the Tigers' win over the Demon Deacons. It was one of four tackles in the game for Wilkins. (Jeremy Brevard/ USA TODAY Sports)

CLEMSON 56, SOUTH CAROLINA 7
November 26, 2016 • Clemson, South Carolina

Clemson Starters Get Rest After All In Blowout of USC

Tigers Thrash Gamecocks for Third Consecutive Win in Series

By Brad Senkiw

Dabo Swinney was asked early in the week by a media member if the Clemson coach was going to sit some of his starters against South Carolina since the Tigers have potentially huge games down the road.

Swinney responded with laughter, called this rivalry showdown "the biggest game of the year" and told the questionnaire, "You're obviously not from South Carolina."

Well, as it turned out, many of Clemson's regulars did get some time off Saturday – by the third quarter.

The No. 3 Tigers built a 35-0 halftime lead and handed the Gamecocks a 56-7 thrashing at Memorial Stadium to end the regular season.

"I'm very happy for our fans," Swinney said. "We know the importance of this game and how everyone lives with the results all year. I'm very happy for our players, especially our seniors. For them to finish the regular season like this is incredible. This was a dominant performance. What a way for these seniors to go out. They were ready from the opening snap."

The only time USC lost worse than this to Clemson was 51-0 in 1900. It was the second highest point total scored in the series by Clemson (11-1), which recorded its third winning streak of at least three games since 1997.

"We knew they weren't in our league," Clemson linebacker Ben Boulware said. "We knew we were going to go out there and dominate them."

Deshaun Watson threw for six touchdowns, the most by a Clemson QB in the series, and tied his own record for the most in school history in a single game. He added 347 passing yards on 26-of-32 passing in just three quarters of play to make sure the Tigers suffered no letdown before next week's ACC Championship game against Virginia Tech.

Clemson WR Mike Williams was the beneficiary of three of those touchdowns, and the junior finished with 100 yards on six catches to help the Tigers stay in the hunt for a spot in the College Football Playoff.

A week after reaching bowl eligibility, South Carolina (6-6) was completely overmatched in every way. The Gamecocks had just 7 yards and zero first downs in the first quarter.

"Not a lot to say. We got beat tonight by a better team," Muschamp said. "I don't know what else to say.

Running back Wayne Gallman leaps over South Carolina defensive lineman D.J. Wonnum during the second quarter of Clemson's 56-7 triumph. Gallman racked up 112 yards and a touchdown on 19 carries in the win. (Ken Ruinard/Independent Mail)

They have a good team across all three phases. We got whipped. On the road recruiting, that's the way we need to change our program."

The Tigers say they were sparked by comments USC made earlier in the week, and there was trash talking and animosity on the field before the game even began, when a skirmish nearly broke out during warmups. USC linebacker Bryson Allen-Williams said one of Clemson's offensive line used a racial slur that started the incident.

"It's irrelevant now," Allen-Williams said. "The score was what it was. Like I said, we've just got to go out there and win the next one."

Clemson improved to 68-42-4 in the series.

"South Carolina has been and always will be the little brother in this rivalry," Boulware said.

The Gamecocks finished with 218 yards, and freshman QB Jake Bentley, who left the game at halftime, finished 7-of-17 passing for 41 yards and one interception. Muschamp said Bentley suffered a leg injury.

"He's fine. No structural issue. I didn't feel good putting him back in," Muschamp said.

Meanwhile, the Tigers moved the ball up and down the field all night, collecting 622 total yards of offense, most in a game against USC, and a school-record 40 first downs.

"Our defense was tremendous all night," Swinney said. "Offensively, we dropped a couple of touchdown passes, but overall we played great. We ran the ball, dominated the line of scrimmage and came away with 40 first downs.

"Deshaun was unbelievable. He played lights out. We were able to sub a lot in the third quarter, and all those guys played well. I'm really proud of our preparation. What a great night for football."

In a game eerily similar to the 2003 63-17 beat down by the Tigers in Columbia, Clemson wasted no time

asserting itself in Death Valley, scoring at least 21 points in the initial quarter for the second consecutive game.

Watson connected with Williams on touchdown passes of 34 and 19 yards before finding tight end Jordan Leggett for an 11-yard scoring strike. All three TDs came against USC defensive back Jamarcus King.

Wayne Gallman, who rushed for 112 yards on 19 carries, had an 8-yard TD in the second quarter, and Williams made it 35-0 at the half after grabbing a 16-yard TD pass from Watson with eight seconds left.

It was an even more comfortable margin than in 2003, when the Tigers led 35-10.

The Gamecocks' only score came on a trick play, when Deebo Samuel threw a receiver pass to Bryan Edwards for a 33-yard touchdown.

The only time Watson and many other starters stepped on the field in the fourth quarter was when they purposely came out of the huddle and saluted the crowd, but never took a snap, instead enjoying what was the final moment in Death Valley for several seniors and juniors moving on to pursue pro careers.

"We're division champs and state champs, and now we're looking to be ACC champs," said Swinney, whose team plays in Orlando next Saturday. "Virginia Tech will be tough, but we're looking for our 16th ACC title. There's still a lot of opportunity left for us. It's fun when you can see the finish line. We're going to empty our tank this week and get ready for a tough Virginia Tech team." ■

Deshaun Watson smiles to the crowd after throwing his sixth touchdown pass to receiver Artavis Scott during the third quarter against South Carolina. In addition to the six touchdowns, Watson tossed for 347 yards in the superb performance. (Ken Ruinard/Independent Mail)

#4 QUARTERBACK
DESHAUN WATSON

Clemson Signal Caller Remembers His Roots

By Scott Keepfer • August 28, 2016

Danny Dunagan, the mayor of Gainesville, has more than a year remaining on his term, which means he won't be facing a challenge from Deshaun Watson anytime soon.

"I would hate to have him as an opponent," Dunagan confessed. "I'm afraid I might lose that one."

Dunagan can probably breathe easy.

It's highly unlikely that Watson, Clemson University's junior quarterback, has designs on a political future just yet – not with a third season with the Tigers and a professional football career looming – but while he may not be the next mayor of this city of 36,306 in north-central Georgia, he darn sure owns the key to the city's heart.

"He's a legend, for sure," says Leslie Frierson, Watson's fourth-grade teacher and now principal at Centennial Arts Academy. "I'll have kids stop me in the hallway and say, 'Did you really teach Deshaun Watson?'

"So yes, he's a celebrity. He's somebody the kids can look at and know that he was a real person who walked these halls, who worked hard and is making a huge impact."

The best way to get to know Deshaun Watson is to spend some time with the people who know him best – namely, the folks in his hometown who marveled at his immense talents on the field and admired his demeanor off it. Watson has earned lofty status in the city's collective consciousness in both regards.

Gainesville has produced numerous athletes of considerable renown, including pitcher Cris Carpenter, a first-round pick in the 1987 Major League Baseball draft, and quarterback Billy Lothridge, runner-up to Roger Staubach for the 1963 Heisman Trophy, but it's hard to imagine any former Gainesville High Red Elephant – past, present or future – being held in the same regard as Watson.

When Watson attended the Heisman Trophy ceremony in New York this past December, he wore a red suit as a nod to his alma mater, further endearing himself to the local populace. "I liked the way he said,

Deshaun Watson has made it look easy on the football field, from his high school days in Gainesville to his record-setting run at Clemson. (Bart Boatwright/The Greenville News)

'This is where it all started,'" said Bruce Miller, his football coach at Gainesville. "Deshaun will never forget his roots, and that showed it."

It seems a safe bet that his hometown will never forget him, either.

Early Star

Watson may have cemented his future by starting at quarterback in his freshman year at Gainesville and as a junior leading the Red Elephants to the 2012 state title – the first in program history – but his legend was born on the playgrounds of his youth.

"I don't think there ever was a time before he was a football star; he was a football star when he was in the fourth grade," Frierson said. "He was incredible. Anyone who had the time to watch him play, they just knew there was something special about him.

"He's always been so smart and able to look at the field and know what he needed to do. He just had this innate sense that was mesmerizing to watch."

After playing outside linebacker as a junior varsity eighth-grader, Watson flashed his potential as a quarterback in the spring before his freshman year, completing 22 of 25 passes in the varsity's spring game.

"It kind of made my decision easy," Miller said.

Watson started the first game of the season, a 14-year-old freshman getting the nod against powerful Buford. Gainesville lost, but Watson threw three touchdown passes in the defeat and jump-started his burgeoning reputation.

"From the get-go it was evident that there was something truly special about the young man," said Katie B. Davis, a former Gainesville High basketball and softball standout who hosts a sports talk radio show – "Game On" – in Gainesville. "He never backed down, already seemed to have a great grasp of the offense and then there was that element of no fear. He was a remarkable athlete, and you knew it from that very first game."

Watson would go on to lead Gainesville to a state title two years later while earning Gatorade Player of the Year honors and becoming the Peach State's all-time passing leader.

He also was a standout in basketball, once scoring 21 points on seven 3-pointers – in the fourth quarter of a game. Miller contends that Watson could have been the state high jump champion if they had been able to convince him to join the track team.

But despite all of the accomplishments, honors and awards, Watson remained the humble, level-headed guy who always seemed to put others first.

Many in town credit his family, and in particular his mother, Deann, for instilling a sense of honor and respect that remains the cornerstone of Deshaun's personality.

"He's homegrown," Miller said. "From a very special family."

In short, Watson has never been about himself, and there is overwhelming evidence to support that contention.

Like the time in the state championship game when he ignored the call from the sideline and changed the play from a quarterback keeper to a handoff so a younger teammate could forever savor the moment he scored a touchdown in a title game.

Or the time when after the title game he remained on the field rather than join many of his teammates on stage for the trophy presentation because "it's for the seniors, and I'm not a senior."

Or the day when Frierson's nephew, Max Williams, declared that his fourth birthday party was going to be a "Deshaun Watson Party," and Watson, who happened to be home on spring break, showed up for the event, making the memory of a lifetime for the birthday boy.

Dual Loyalties

Gainesville is University of Georgia country, so it's no surprise that the high school's "G" and red-and-black

Deshaun Watson's jersey hangs in the concession stand at Gainesville High's Bobby Gruhn Field in Gainesville, Georgia. Watson led the Red Elephants to the school's only state championship during his junior season. (Bart Boatwright/The Greenville News)

colors mirror those of the university located just 40 miles away. But Watson, who decided to cast his lot with Clemson early in his high school career, has in many instances transcended the loyalties of the local fan base.

Frierson, a Georgia alum and self-professed Bulldogs diehard, had her heart put to the test a couple of years ago when Clemson played in Athens, Georgia, in the 2014 season opener.

"I was at the game, and when Deshaun threw his first touchdown pass, I cried I was so excited for him," Frierson said. "It was incredible to watch this – in my eyes, 9-year-old kid – who was commanding the field and owning it. I had on my red and black, but I was cheering for Deshaun all day.

"I tell people now that in our family we bleed red and black. And Deshaun orange."

Such is a common refrain in Gainesville.

"Yeah, it's Georgia territory, but now it's Clemson territory, too," Miller said. "There are a lot of people in this town that when Clemson and Georgia played, I don't know who they were pulling for. They're Georgia folks, but I think many of them had some dual loyalties going on."

Wayne Vickery, who was Gainesville High's athletic director during Watson's four years, made the trek to Glendale, Arizona, this past January to see Watson and Clemson square off against Alabama.

"I was at the national championship game," Vickery said. "I flew from Greenville and back in one day. I thought hunting season was open, there was so much orange on that plane."

Gainesville native Tommy Aaron, a longtime PGA Tour pro and winner of the 1973 Masters, didn't fly to Arizona and wasn't sporting orange, but tuned in with keen interest.

"I was pulling for Clemson and Deshaun," Aaron said. "He's quite an amazing player. It's unbelievable what he can do. It doesn't look like he's doing much when he's running with the ball, but all of a sudden you look up and he's gained 20 yards."

Vickery and Aaron are regulars at Gainesville's Longstreet Café, which is one of Watson's favorite local eateries, and every now and then there are mornings at the restaurant when the consumption of scrambled eggs and grits and biscuits and gravy comes to a screeching halt.

Those are the days when Watson strolls into his favorite hometown eatery, where his framed No. 4 Gainesville High football jersey gazes down upon the customers, a reminder of glory past and glory to come.

"When Deshaun comes in, there's a buzz that he's here and everybody wants an autograph or a picture," said Tim Bunch, the restaurant's owner. "He doesn't get much time to himself, but he's willing to accommodate anybody who asks."

Such is life for Gainesville's hometown hero, who remains a somewhat reluctant one.

The understated Watson has never sought the spotlight, but the glow couldn't help but find him given the victories and trophies and record-breaking Saturdays that have become commonplace under his command.

"I'm not surprised by anything he's done," Davis said. "If he didn't have the work ethic he has, if he didn't have the type of personality he has, if he wasn't the kind of man he is, then maybe we'd all be a little more shocked.

"But his work ethic is second to none and his love for his family, his love for his community, and his love for his coaches, teammates and friends is second to none. When you've got somebody like that, it's not shocking that he's been as successful as he's been. And I can't wait to see what he does this year. It's going to be pretty remarkable."

As Watson prepares for what will most certainly be his final season at Clemson, his presence and popularity is at an all-time high, not only in Gainesville, but far beyond.

He's an overwhelming favorite to repeat as Atlantic

Watson in the Georgia Dome after leading the Red Elephants to the school's only state championship. He was destined for gridiron greatness from a young age. (Provided Photo)

Coast Conference Player of the Year and is the primary reason the No. 2-ranked team in the nation harbors hopes of finishing No. 1.

Frierson says that seeing Watson everywhere she turns – on TV, magazine covers, at the Heisman Trophy ceremony – seems somewhat surreal.

"I just want to cry most of the time," Frierson said. "Because I look at all of the things he's doing and I know what his dreams were when he was in the fourth grade, and he's living them, and that's the most exciting thing of all to watch. We're just so proud of him."

And how about that Gainesville mayoral race that could unfold many years hence?

"By the time Deshaun gets out of pro ball, I'll be long retired by then," Mayor Dunagan said. "But we'd be lucky to have him as mayor, I'll tell you that." ■

ACC CHAMPIONSHIP GAME

CLEMSON 42, VIRGINIA TECH 35
December 3, 2016 • Orlando, Florida

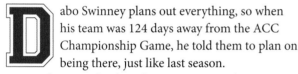

Another ACC Title, and Now Another Playoff Run?

Clemson Heads to College Football Playoff Looking for Revenge

By Brad Senkiw

Dabo Swinney plans out everything, so when his team was 124 days away from the ACC Championship Game, he told them to plan on being there, just like last season.

At that time, he thought it was going to be in Charlotte, but the No. 3 Tigers' road to what they believe will be another College Football Playoff berth took a little detour through Orlando, Florida.

A change of venue, and a feisty Virginia Tech squad that never wanted to go away, weren't enough to derail Clemson's road to what appears to be a return to the College Football Playoff.

ACC title game MVP Deshaun Watson accounted for five touchdowns for the Tigers, who held off Virginia Tech for a 42-35 victory in front of 50,628 fans.

"I'm proud of our guys, though. I'm proud of our team," Swinney said. "Happy for our seniors, happy for our fans. This was special. You know, this is our fourth appearance and our third title. And they're all special. Every one of them is kind of its own story. It was its own journey."

Virginia Tech QB Jerod Evans had three touchdowns on the night and kept the Hokies in the game. But

Clemson's defense, which bent and broke at times in the final quarter, turned the Hokies over at the Clemson 14-yard line with 1:11 left in the game to seal the program's 16th ACC championship, which passes Florida State in the conference, and third of the Swinney era.

Clemson (12-1) became just the third team in school history to reach 12 wins in a single season.

The Tigers won back-to-back conference titles for the first time since Danny Ford led them to three consecutive championships from 1986-88.

"Both times it was pretty sweet, but I think this one is more sweet because it's something we haven't done in 28 years, win back-to-back championships, and we really had to earn it," Watson said. "A lot of guys just putting out the work, and just the senior class being able to step in and win our 47th game in our career and, you know, get the ACC Championship. So both was pretty sweet, but I think this one was just a little bit sweeter just because of that reason."

It was a celebration not seen by nearly as many fans as last year, when 74,514 witnessed Clemson's 2015 championship in Charlotte, but a change in venue because of political reasons didn't stop the Tigers from

Deshaun Watson holds the ACC championship trophy after Clemson's 42-35 win over Virginia Tech. Watson – the MVP of the game – accounted for five touchdowns, threw for 288 yards and rushed for 85 yards. (Bart Boatwright/The Greenville News)

dropping 470 yards of offense in Orlando.

The No. 19 Hokies (9-4), in their first year with head coach Justin Fuente at the helm, racked up 162 of their 386 total yards in the fourth quarter and wore down the Tigers' defense.

Clemson was up seven and facing a second-and-19 at the CU 16 in the fourth quarter before Hunter Renfrow made a leaping 31-yard catch. After a pair of false starts gave Clemson a third-and-14, Deon Cain high-pointed a pass and came down with it for 30 yards.

"I knew I had pressure from the field, so I just kind of rode to my left because it was just about time to get Deon Cain off the release, and I just gave him a shot," said Watson, who hung in the pocket and took a hit to deliver the pass.

On the next play, Watson faked a run on a sprint out and tossed a short pass to Renfrow, who raced 15 yards into the end zone for a 35-21 Clemson advantage with 7:33 left in the game.

But guess what? It didn't last. The Hokies matched it with a six-play, 76-yard touchdown drive to get back within a touchdown and set up a dramatic finish.

Opposite: Wayne Gallman carried the ball 17 times for 59 yards against Virginia Tech. (Bart Boatwright/The Greenville News) Above: Deshaun Watson hugs wide receiver Deon Cain after a Clemson touchdown in the third quarter. (Bart Boatwright/The Greenville News)

"Obviously, we came up a little short but it wasn't because we weren't out there competing," Fuente said. "I think our kids poured their heart and soul into this and are going to learn some life lessons from this endeavor but I'm awfully proud in the way they believed and the way they prepared and ultimately how they played."

Clemson was unable to pick up a first down on its next possession and gave Tech the ball back with 4:03 to play.

And facing fourth-and-6 at CU 23, Evans was intercepted by Cordrea Tankersley, and the Tigers all but stamped their pass back to the playoff for the second consecutive year.

"We needed a turnover," Tankersley said. "Credit to our defensive line for getting pressure, (forcing) the quarterback to get the ball out quick and our corners just reacted to it, and I give credit to our coaches for having us in the right calls to make those plays."

Up 21-14 at the half, Watson threw an interception on Clemson's first drive of the third quarter, but the Hokies were unable to come away with points.

The Tigers made them pay for that, using a nine-play, 89-yard drive in which they rushed six times and scored on an 8-yard TD run by Wayne Gallman to go up 14.

Clemson extended that lead to three touchdowns on Watson's second rushing score of the night. The Hokies wouldn't go away, though. A 42-yard pass from Evans to Bucky Hodges led to a 27-yard TD run by Travon McMillan to get within two touchdowns.

Clemson marched down the field on its first two drives, scoring on a 3-yard TD run by Watson and a 21-yard pass to Leggett to build a 14-0 lead just nine minutes into the game.

Virginia Tech used a fake punt/lob pass and a pass interference on Clemson DB Cordrea Tankersley to get into Clemson territory and set up a 1-yard TD run by Travon McMillan to make it 14-7 with 51 seconds left in the first quarter.

Dabo Swinney hoists the ACC Championship trophy after his Tigers defeated Virginia Tech, his third such trophy as the coach of the Tigers. (Bart Boatwright/The Greenville News)

Clemson's offense continued its torrid start when Watson found Leggett again for a 10-yard TD pass with 11:46 left in the half, but the Hokies upped their pressure after that and began laying some hits on Watson.

That slowed Clemson's attack, and Evans got the Hokies within 21-14 on an 11-yard TD run about four minutes before the half.

"There's a reason why it's been that long," Swinney said about winning back-to-back ACC titles. "It's hard to do. And these guys set out to do that at the beginning of the year, and they were all brought here for this moment, we all were, and it's just awesome to be a part of seeing a group of young people come together, lay it on the line for one another, and just play their guts out all year long." ∎

Opposite: The Tigers celebrate their 42-35 win over Virginia Tech in the ACC Championship at Camping World Stadium in Orlando. (Bart Boatwright/The Greenville News) Above: Defensive lineman Clelin Ferrell (99) celebrates with defensive lineman Christian Wilkins (42) after a defensive stop against Virginia Tech during the first quarter of the ACC Championship. Ferrell had six tackles on the day, including a sack. (Bart Boatwright/The Greenville News)

FIESTA BOWL

CLEMSON 31, OHIO STATE 0
December 31, 2016 • Glendale, Arizona

Defense Leads Charge to Clemson's National Championship Game Return

Offense Also Had Stellar Game as Deshaun Watson Shows Off

By Brad Senkiw

So much talk heading into the College Football Playoff's semifinal Fiesta Bowl surrounded Clemson quarterback Deshaun Watson and a talented receiving corps, and how it would match up with the vaunted Ohio State defense.

But as the saying goes, defense wins championships. For Clemson, it's why it gets another shot at one.

The Tigers (13-1) won Saturday night's playoff game 31-0 to earn a rematch with undefeated Alabama in the national championship game.

"What a night. What a journey," Clemson head coach Dabo Swinney said. "I just can't tell you how proud I am of our team, our staff. Incredible resolve. Relentless pursuit to get back here and find a way to win."

At University of Phoenix Stadium, the Tigers' stop unit stopped the Buckeyes (11-2) all night and served them their first shutout since 1993 and the first of head coach Urban Meyer's career.

"They have great players, a great offense, great quarterback, great athletes," Clemson linebacker Kendall Joseph said. "We prepared hard but a shutout is rare. For us to do that shows we worked really hard and it paid off for us."

And much like the Crimson Tide, which beat Washington 24-7 in the Peach Bowl semifinal on Saturday, Clemson did it with defense against the Buckeyes. The Tigers held Ohio State to 215 total yards and nine first downs. An offense that came into the game averaging 258 rushing yards per game gained 88 yards.

"I'm not surprised at all," said Clemson cornerback Cordrea Tankersley, who had an interception in the game. "The work that we've put in since last January, it doesn't surprise me at all that we won big.

"I feel like we were (overlooked). We wanted to go out and play our game and not worry about Ohio State."

Clemson produced 11 tackles for a loss and forced two turnovers as the defensive line dominated the Buckeyes and made life miserable for QB J.T. Barrett.

Deshaun Watson runs for a touchdown against Ohio State during the third quarter of the College Football Playoff semifinal game in the Fiesta Bowl. Watson scored three touchdowns in Clemson's 31-0 rout of Ohio State. (David Kadlubowski/The Republic)

Senior defensive tackle Carlos Watkins and redshirt freshman defensive end Clelin Ferrell spent much of the night wreaking havoc in the backfield. Watkins recorded a pair of sacks to give him 10.5, breaking the school record for sacks in a season by a defensive tackle shared by William Perry (1984) and Michael Dean Perry (1987).

Ferrell was a monster, finishing with three tackles for a loss and a sack to earn Fiesta Bowl Defensive MVP honors.

"Hats off to my teammates, my coaches and we realize we're playing for something bigger than ourselves and that's the best fans in the country," Ferrell said. "I'm just happy I got the opportunity to help my team tonight."

The Tiger offense was pretty sharp too, finishing with 470 total yards, the most Ohio State's allowed this year. Clemson ended up getting all the points it needed in the first quarter when Greg Huegel hit a 45-yard field goal on the Tigers' first drive before Watson punched in a TD on a 1-yard run with 2:16 left in the first for a 10-0 lead.

Opposite: Defensive end Clelin Ferrell (far left) is named defensive player of the game in the Fiesta Bowl. Ferrell had three tackles for loss on the day, including a sack. (Cheryl Evans/azcentral sports) Above: A young Clemson fan celebrates as Clemson trounces Ohio State to advance to the national championship game. (Rob Schumacher/azcentral sports)

Watson rushed for another score in the third quarter and tossed a 30-yard TD to C.J. Fuller in the second quarter. The star quarterback finished the game with 316 total yards.

"It was an overall team effort," Swinney said.

And by the second half, the Tigers had worn down Ohio State and started racking up big chunks of yards. Wayne Gallman rushed for 64 of his 85 yards in the final 30 minutes and added a touchdown after Van Smith picked off a Barrett pass in the end zone and returned it 86 yards in the fourth quarter.

For Clemson, a very slight underdog at kickoff, it was another impressive bowl win over a storied program. Since 2012, the Tigers have beaten LSU, Ohio State and Oklahoma in the postseason.

"I'm just happy to get a win here in Arizona. I got my butt kicked as a player in 1990 and obviously we lost last year (to Alabama in Glendale)," said Swinney.

For Meyer, it was just his third loss in 13 bowl appearances, but second to the Tigers in the last four

Opposite: Offensive MVP Deshaun Watson celebrates the resounding Clemson victory after the game. (Rob Schumacher/azcentral sports) Above: Clemson running back C.J. Fuller catches a touchdown during the second quarter of the 31-0 win. Fuller had three receptions for 45 yards in the game. (Rob Schumacher/azcentral sports)

years. Even one of the winningest college football coaches of any era, and owner of three national titles, couldn't figure out how to get his offense going against this defense.

"Defensively, really indescribable," Swinney said. "It was guys getting their tails ready to play and then winning their matchups. Outside of a couple of plays… we really played a clean game."

The Tigers ran the blueprint to stopping this offense perfectly. They shut down the run and took away short passes on early downs and forced Barrett to beat them on third-and-longs. With a defensive front that was teeing off, it kept OSU from gaining any momentum and forced Ohio State to throw 33 times and run just 23, while Barrett completed 57 percent of his throws.

"That was not the game plan," Meyer said. "We kind of got taken out of the game plan. We wanted to be balanced if we had stuck to the plan." ■

Opposite: Defensive tackle Albert Huggins (67) grabs the jersey of Ohio State quarterback J.T. Barrett as he scrambles during the fourth quarter. Barrett struggled mightily in the game, throwing for only 127 yards, no touchdowns and two interceptions. (Rob Schumacher/ azcentral sports) Above: Dabo Swinney celebrates after Clemson defeated Ohio State to advance to the national championship game for the second consecutive season. (David Kadlubowski/The Republic)

Clemson running back Wayne Gallman escapes the grasp of Ohio State linebacker Raekwon McMillan during the second quarter of Clemson's triumph. Gallman had 85 yards on 18 carries and a touchdown. (Cheryl Evans/azcentral sports)

CHAMPION